Triumph After Trauma

11 Keys to Positive Parenting After Trauma

Christy Copeland

Triumph After Trauma: 11 Keys to Positive Parenting After Trauma
First published 2018

For permission requests, write to the author via email:
ccopeland@leaderswellnesssuite.com.

Bulk Ordering Information
Special discounts are available on quantity purchases by corporations, associations and others. For details, contact the author at the address above.

Printed in the United States of America

Cover by Jabez Design & Marketing
Edited by Renée Purdie, Rising Star Entrepreneurial Enterprises LLC
Formatted by Polgarus Studio

Dedication

This book is dedicated to Mrs. Lillie M. Greene, my eighth-grade teacher. The best teachers are those who inspire.

This book is also dedicated to my dear children, as well as the inner child of every soul who will read this book. May you find the golden nuggets in your story to move you forward to victory.

Contents

Acknowledgements

Giving honor to God the Father and my Lord and Savior Jesus Christ and the precious gift of the Holy Spirit who makes it possible for me to live the overcoming life and to share my journey to encourage others.

To the gifts who helped to make this book possible: Demetrius, Isaac, Christyna, Jonathan, Diane, Tellies, Sr., Tellies, Jr., Anthony, Beatrice, Teleisa and Jacori. Thank you for allowing me time away from you to birth this book. To my grandparents whose unconditional love was evident throughout my life. You inspire me to live fully and I am grateful. To my editor, Renée Purdie, for your expertise, encouragement and persistence. Thank you for helping me to communicate my heart to everyone who will read this book. To Jaiyde Walters and Jabez Design and Marketing for interpreting my imagination in visual form. To Vanessa Collins and Sean Smith for your continued support. To my pastors, Drs. William Winston and Veronica Winston for their commitment to impart knowledge and faith to people everywhere. To the spiritual leaders who share their knowledge, experience and resources with my family. To the business leaders who have demonstrated discipline, vulnerability and courage. Thank you for your training, inspiration and allowing me to use my gifts to serve you freely and speak into your life. To my family and friends who continue to provide inspiration and encouragement on this journey.

Foreword

Christy Copeland is an ordained Minister of the Gospel of Jesus Christ, a Prophetic Psalmist, a Modern Day Visionary, and an Amazing Parent after Trauma. The energy, excitement and power she utilizes to encourage the people of God, on a daily basis, continues to amaze me. Christy is a gracious encourager, an effective writer and a dynamic instrument of God awakening us to areas that we would sometimes prefer to overlook and pretend they never existed. Christy has been raised up, by the Lord, for such a time as this. A time when everyone's focus is being turned towards inward health and mental stability and the effects they have on all concerned.

In Triumph After Trauma: 11 Keys to Positive Parenting After Trauma, Christy inspires and motivates her readers to a bold commitment to look deep within, in an effort to grow. Also, to gather the strength to persists, even in the face of adversity, deep hurt, domestic violence and rejection. Every single page has provocative insights on how to move forward with "Positive Parenting" while experiencing hardship. This book is written to inspire perseverance utilizing powerful scriptural references and principles.

"Triumph After Trauma: 11 Keys to Positive Parenting After Trauma" is amazingly impactful and insightful. It will serve its purpose of guiding anyone who reads it to reflect with a renewed sense of perspective. A perspective that will inspire instead of condemn; that will cause you to move forward and no longer remain stagnant; that will move you beyond your comfort zone of lack and worries, to more than enough and power.

"Triumph After Trauma: 11 Keys to Positive Parenting After Trauma" is filled with real life issues and concerns that we, as parents, refuse to speak about and/or address. But, Christy boldly tackles each and every situation imaginable, with grace and courage. She holds back nothing in an effort to empower "the many". In the book she addresses 11 key issues gained through her own personal life experiences. And even though this book was written for "parents", many of the keys will benefit anyone who has experienced betrayal, deception, domestic violence, "church hurt," abandonment and/or spiritual or personal bondage.

This book is equipped with 11 Keys that have been researched and expounded upon to empower the reader. Each Key is backed by scriptural references and written to insure the reader has a clear understanding of how to utilize them. Christy also gives insight on utilizing our spiritual weapons, not only to combat the enemy and his devices, but to utterly destroy him.

You will be captivated by the message of "Triumph After Trauma: 11 Keys to Positive Parenting After Trauma"," and compelled to actively participate in life and fulfill your destiny in spite of relational, inter-personal and/or inner-personal challenges. You will be inspired in knowing that any troubles that you have encountered in life, significantly pales to the strength that lies within you.

Christy has stirred my spiritual emotions, as I ventured with her through this book. It caused me to reflect on the experiences and life challenges that I have encountered. I was moved to look at the things that I had experienced with renewed eyes; helping me to realize that each experience was always meant to be a part of my "His-story". Necessary experiences I had to tackle to move me closer to "Me". Necessary things I had to experience to move me closer to "Thee".

May this book be used to inspire, motivate and help equip every reader to overcome any obstacle that is encountered. To empower each of you to move forward in life and make full proof of the strengths that lie inside of you. And, finally, to encourage each of you to achieve your Kingdom purpose that you were created to fulfill in the earth realm.

Peace!!

Prophetess Dr. Deborah Cullins-Threets
Founder and President
Kingdom Developmental Institute

Introduction

> For I know the plans I have for you," says the LORD. "They are plans for good and not for disaster, to give you a future and a hope. Jeremiah 29:11 New Living Translation

Do you know where your child is at the moment? Do you know what is on the mind of your child? How do you define parenting after trauma?

Active parenting remains relevant today and will be in the days to come regardless of the advancement of technology or world affairs. We are moving faster as a society, but we fall behind in emotional health. The number of reports of young adolescents committing suicide is climbing. Juvenile detention centers are overcrowded and there are plans to build more (and more) prisons. More children are being charged as adults. One study showed that opioids are the leading cause of overdose among teens of wealthy families. A news reports showed that since 2013, every week there is a shooting when school is in session across America. Adding to the concerns, social media makes it challenging for parents to keep up with who is influencing the behaviors of our children.

This book is a response to conversations I have had with numerous family members and friends as we explore new territory as single parents. According to a November 2016 U.S. Census Bureau report, there are 17.3 million children in America who live with their mother only and 3 Million children who live with their father only. We know that not all single parents are victims of abuse and unfortunate circumstances that are then passed on to their children. However, this book is meant to help any parent leader who struggles emotionally, mentally and physically to move forward after trauma, such as a painful divorce, sickness or death of loved one, abandonment and broken expectations.

Post-traumatic stress Disorder (PTSD), according to the U.S. National Library of Medicine, is an anxiety disorder that some people develop after experiencing a shocking, scary or dangerous event. The term is more popular to describe an event of military combat. However, it also develops in reaction to physical injury or severe mental or emotional distress, including: violent assault, natural disaster or other life-threatening events.

Some of our children suffer from identity confusion because we define who we are by the reactions of pain. Therefore, we plant and cultivate doubt, fear and unbelief with our speech and behavior. It is often the posture of disappointment of the unhappily ever after.

We hide behind fortresses that do not serve us nor our family. The fortress of our career demands huge blocks of our time and attention away and does not allow us to have heart conversations with those who need us most. After all, we are obligated to work, right? We toss our child cash or a credit card to purchase lesser things that can never replace us. We don't realize that we send them out to a cold, cruel world unprepared emotionally—a world that may exploit his gifts without nurturing the value of who he is. She walks with her head down, unsure of her true potential. Your young adult accepts jobs that do not fit his natural talents. He may get into the top school, but he is driven more by his desire to rebel against you for neglect.

One young man became an attorney because his dad was a very successful attorney. He thought it would bring his father closer to him. His father was proud and used his connections to ensure he had a great job waiting for him. But the relationship between them did not change all that much. He was miserable so he chose another field.

Our children choose friends who seem to have more influence than us. They are searching for something to heal their pain. Yes, our children are hurting. How does a child become hopeless when they have material wealth and the best that money can buy? Do they lose value or do we never teach or model their value?

Parenting is "farming" work. We look to different sources such as books, television, tradition and search engines for answers hoping the soil will produce a bountiful crop. The harvest does not show up right away. There are unpleasant smells, attitudes, misunderstandings, insults on our character as parents, bold truth and mistakes. Lots of mistakes. Scripture says to endure hardness as a good soldier. Some parents give up during the difficult seasons. Some sow seeds on hard ground because our walk doesn't back up the talk. But every season is meaningful.

The English Standard Version of Psalm 127, verse 3, states, "Children are a heritage from the Lord, they are a reward from him." How many babies are dropped off at hospitals, fire stations or are shuffled between foster care homes? Some parents check out mentally or choose substance abuse to escape what seems overwhelming and much too hard to bear. The good news is a worthy investment of time and energy in this assignment can give you many years of pleasure that money cannot buy.

This book is also for the married person who feels like a single parent because the other parent, for whatever reason, has taken their hands off this great responsibility. When a child runs into trouble, the other parent does not show up.

There are parents who struggle with low-paying jobs, past due notices who must actively seek financial supplements for food and housing. There are parents who have years of work experience and oversee departments and organizations but suffer in silence. They feel it is expected for them to keep going without proper acknowledgement of the trauma that has changed their lives forever.

Parents from all walks of life and socio-economic backgrounds, races and cultures can choose to take courage and create a peaceful life for you and your child after trauma. I applaud you for making the decision to pick up this book. There is hope with your participation. Your best life is waiting. Your child deserves a better tomorrow as you take courage to adopt beliefs that support your growth and strengthen the core of your family bond.

Using my own journey and the lessons I have learned by trial, error and revelation, I have set forth these 11 keys that will ignite your path from the symptoms of what feels like Post-Traumatic Stress Disorder (PTSD) to a different PTSD: Parent Transforming with Strength and Dominion.

Are you ready? Let's get started!

CHAPTER ONE

What Just Happened?

> Look straight ahead and fix your eyes on what lies before you. Proverbs 4:25 New Living Translation

Trauma is defined as a deeply distressing or disturbing experience. This can include the emotional and psychological trauma involved in the breakup of a significant relationship which is a humiliating or deeply disappointing experience. If we have not properly acknowledged them, our emotions are just as raw as when it first happened. Emotions buried alive do not die. Stop and process.

Despite the widely held belief, time alone does not heal all wounds. Whether it is 30 days, 30 months or 30 years, some of us parents get stuck in our story or our version of the story. We are left with mental paralysis, heartache and sometimes physical pain. Like a movie, we replay some parts and forget other parts. We tend to park, like a vehicle, on what was done to us or what we did or did not do. Perhaps you are trained to view crying as a sign of weakness. "Be strong and keep going," they say. You may be afraid of your emotions for fear of not recovering. But to ignore this moment will negatively impact your life span. There is another option and a better life waiting.

Somewhat crippled, we as parents must find strength to care for our little ones. How do I raise a child in this world when I feel like crap? How do I escape the pain and abandonment and find a reason to live? How do I find hope in a hopeless situation?

Some of us go back into a toxic relationship because a different road is unfamiliar and uncomfortable. Parent leader, be strengthened today. Press through the difficulty of broken expectation. If not for you right now, press through for your child.

Would you believe that many men and women attempt to minimize the reactions of these life-altering events? If you give yourself to someone emotionally and physically and they reject you or they die, there is loss. There is a tear in the fabric of your life. The reaction to trauma may go undiagnosed, or there are accusations and judgments of the traumatic events. At the suggestion of well-meaning friends and family, you may be tempted to go on a date or maintain the other parts of your life as if little or nothing has happened. It is the other person's loss, you may say with your lips, but nothing can soothe the awful ache of your broken heart. You may be dealing with rejection and low self-esteem. Stop and process.

If we skip this part, we begin on a rocky road of over-reacting to similar emotional triggers in other areas of our lives. We may be short on patience with our child. We may attempt to pour all of the pain into a new relationship. We cut and paste others into roles that ignore who they are in an attempt to mend that sore part of us. We numb out and go from one relationship to another leaving our children vulnerable to the cruelty of others. I read a news report that a twenty-three-year-old man dumped his girlfriend's 19-month-old daughter in a forest. She had been assaulted with head injuries while the mother's boyfriend was babysitting her. Hurting people hurt people.

What are the facts of your story? If you only deal with how you feel and not the facts, this stage is incomplete.

My story

I was born in Detroit, Michigan where my maternal grandparents lived. After a year of marriage, my parents moved to my father's hometown, the Bronzeville neighborhood of Chicago, Illinois and then to their own home. I was raised in a middle-class home on the south side in the seventies: the era of Soul Train, bell bottoms, Jays Potato Chips, Gladys Soul Food Restaurant, while hearing the music of Andre Crouch and Dr. Charles G. Hayes & the Cosmopolitan Church of Prayer radio broadcast. While growing up, I have witnessed the reign of the first woman mayor, the honorable Jane M. Byrne and the first African American mayor, the honorable Harold Washington. I am the oldest of three children. While I honor my parents for their efforts, I am comfortable to say we were sheltered as children. I was fortunate to have access to both of my parents growing up.

I remember riding the school bus to school in my earlier years. And then after my father graduated college, I rode to our church school with my Dad, a passionate educator. He was also a minister and attempted to live by the strict rules of his church organization that even he had difficulty following. He would never admit that though which makes me sad. To have a conversation with him about his religious doctrine was to agree, fight or walk away. He loved his parents and attempted to help raise the children of his siblings. He was admired by his students and would have extremely long conversations with the people he called friends while my brother and I patiently stood nearby. We knew not to join "grown folk" conversation. My parents believed in children being seen and not heard. Things were easier when we quickly obeyed. Rarely did they allow me to express my thoughts so my limited insight as a curious child caused much resentment. There was something mysterious about my Dad that kept my attention. He was the first man I ever loved. He was a comical soul when he was calm so it was important that I studied him well so I would know what not to do.

Unfortunately, as I got older I noticed that he became more engrossed in his own thoughts unless I did something wrong. He was moody on most days. I felt like I had to read between the impatient demands and putdowns to determine when to make a request of him. "Clean up!" "You missed that over there. Do it again!" My mother, attentive to his every command also, moved as quietly as she could. When she asked questions about his whereabouts or attempted to impart wisdom, he would roar to discourage her. I heard him say awful things to my mother and his thunderous outbursts at home made me beg my mother in a soft whisper to please don't ask any more questions so he would stop yelling and throwing things. In fact, the entire neighborhood could hear him with windows raised from our modest house with three other houses closely situated. The walk from our house to the car as we were dressed up to go to church was the longest walk ever as I felt the stares of our neighbors. My thought was: "Can I just vanish now?"

Ironically, his pastor would yell and call names too so as a child church seemed like a continuation of the negative energy I experienced at home. I watched my Dad minister from the pulpit to people at various church gatherings in our city, in other states and even at the church my grandfather pastored in Detroit. He labored long with people until he sweated out of his shirts. But when he was done there, he spoke to us from a place of impatient frustration. I wanted to say so badly, "Dad, prophesy: tell me what you see in me. Do you notice anything worthwhile in me?" The question lay quiet in my mind.

Consequently, I thought God was this huge force who judged harshly and frantically wrote down everything I did wrong. I failed at keeping the rules as I understood it. And because my Dad received positive feedback from the people he ministered to, I thought that somehow, he was approved by God for the way he treated us. Is this as good as life gets? Suicidal thoughts hovered over me. I stayed in a posture of inadequacy and worthlessness as I watched in silence.

I would run upstairs to my room and write long letters of what I thought of his treatment of us. And then I would tear it up into tiny pieces so he could never find it. As a child, I used to ponder what about us made him so unhappy. I did not learn until later that my mother earned more although sometimes she did not decide how it was spent. It was her labor that provided our private school education, including my Dad's college education. I am not sure she knew how much he made. We went grocery shopping with him faithfully every two weeks after leaving school.

My mother, who is six years younger than my Dad, worked midnights so she slept almost until it was time to cook and go to work. I believe part of that was despair or depression. We would hide her shoes and keys and beg her not to leave us. She would sit down for a while, but then she would leave anyway. I understand now that it is easier to spend time in places where we are celebrated for our efforts. If we did not get home from school in time, because my Dad would grade papers in his classroom or stay for church service on Tuesday and Friday nights, we would not see my mother for an entire day. It hurt me so much because I needed her. Maybe avoiding each other worked for them, but I needed them. To try to fill the void, I wrote and sang songs.

On weekends, she would provide benevolence to others just like my grandparents did. They approved her marriage to my Dad, a traveling evangelist, so she may have felt she had a duty to stay with him as long as she did. My mother is an excellent musician who learned to play by ear at their church in Detroit. Unfortunately, she never shared her genius with me nor did we practice. However, my parents expected me to confidently sing at church when they called me. I was unprepared and felt unsure of myself. My mother scolded me for acting "high minded."

In 1982, I was swiftly moved out of my seventh-grade classroom into the eighth-grade classroom. My teacher smiled so I thought it might be a good thing, but I was not sure. I was told I would be there for the remainder of the year. I remember trying to understand if my Dad did something wrong or if I did something wrong. Soon came the congratulations and well wishes from everyone. At home, we would spend long hours studying with my Dad. I was a good student, partly because I believed the harsh criticisms of my Dad more than my own ability. Mrs. Lillie Greene was preparing the class for graduation and had assigned parts of the poem written by Dorothy Nolte, entitled "Children Learn What They Live." She had it set to music. The deposit of the entire poem made an unforgettable impact on me.

My days of exploration of the world outside of the silver gate that surrounded our house happened when my parents allowed me to walk home from my Catholic high school. This was not their first plan. My Dad insisted on taking me to school in the morning, but my mother would oversleep when it was time to pick me up. When he asked, I would complain to my Dad about how cold it was to walk during the winter in a skirt. No pants allowed! Mom bought me leg warmers.

Attending a new school was a difficult adjustment for me because my Dad was not down the hall teaching in another classroom, as in the previous years. It was refreshing but I was afraid and did not know what to expect. I was twelve years old in a new environment with older children who had different beliefs and generous freedoms. My grades tumbled as I moved along quietly taking it all in. It was the first time I attended mass and learned that people worship God differently than we did. My parents did not allow me to join sports or activities except the choir. I enjoyed singing lead vocals and I won a Who's Who in Music award.

On the walk home, I was able to scope out the neighborhood for myself. While Dad made sure we were academically astute, I was naive about those streets. He preferred it that way. He said the world is bad and told me to stay away from boys with no discussion. This did not mean I did. It just meant his lack of instructions made me vulnerable to all sorts of mischievousness. My ignorance made me an easy victim. He also made painful remarks about my body that played like a parrot in my head as I attempted to cover up my developing chest. He and the people at his church would call me, "fast." "Sit your fast tail down!" I did not know what the term meant for sure, but I knew it was not a compliment. As I passed by the houses on my way home from school trying to make sense of things, some neighbors spoke and others just stared. By senior year, one young man would always wave.

I graduated from high school at 16 and wanted to go far away to college. My Dad insisted that I enroll in the local university and take the classes of his choice. It was boring and difficult. I told him I wanted to sing and write music, but it was not good enough for him. He said I would never make it in the industry. He said I should be a teacher like him. My mother said I should be a nurse "because there will always be sick people."

At age 18, When my parents divorced, I left school to find a job. We were estranged from my Dad. As I got older, I became more vocal and asked questions. "You had it all" was the lyrics I secretly penned. There was a sense of relief. My promise to myself is that at the age of 18, I would never step into another church again. However, I was unsure if my mother was capable of protecting us as a single parent. As the oldest, I tried to help raise my brothers. It did not help. I cried out to God to help us. I did not believe God would favor us. I did not know who or what would deliver us.

I wandered through downtown Chicago where the museums are. My Dad would often take us to The Art Institute, The Museum of Science & Industry, The Shedd Aquarium and the Lincoln Park Zoo. Although I was sheltered from many things, my Dad provided enough of a glimpse for me to realize there is more in the world to explore. I started to be hopeful about finding my identity and purpose.

I found a temporary job on the Magnificent Mile in downtown Chicago working for the headquarters of William Wrigley Jr. Company. With no administrative experience, these people believed that my friendly personality would open doors. My mother was afraid for me, but she could tell that I was determined. A few years went by and I was hired by Helene Curtis, Inc., a manufacturer of personal care products. The training and positive support shown to me by the people I worked with was surprising and encouraging. I learned about office procedures and etiquette. I eventually purchased my own car. Life at home was not perfect, even with my father gone, but my outlook was brighter.

After some time had passed, I saw the young man that used to wave at me on the way home from school. We stopped for a chat. He was tall, dark and handsome. His grandparents lived around the corner from us for many years. He, along with his Mom and sister, came to live with them after his parent's divorce. He was a part of a huge family who also had houses around us. When I would visit him, I did not give much attention to the sad pictures of him displayed until he told me about his painful childhood later. I invited him to my new less restrictive church with a well-liked pastor, lots of young people and great music. With money to donate offerings, I thought for sure I would find acceptance by what I thought I knew: the church. We sang all the top Gospel songs, had gospel artists stop by and because I sang in the choir, I was able to travel with the pastor. The experiences were great, but it did nothing for my wounded soul.

The young man agreed to visit. Soon, every weekend, he was riding around with me. He was quiet and meditative. He agreed with everything I said. He met my new-found friends who liked him and encouraged our courtship. After six months, he started a labor job with the County.

Because we were involved in sex before marriage, I became consumed with "making it right" according to the fire and brimstone messages I heard my father preach in the pulpit so many times. We got engaged. His mother threw me a bridal shower. My mother refused to support our engagement until a few days before the wedding. My pastor was not immediately available to counsel us. When he did meet with us, it was a week before the wedding and it was brief. I remember so vividly the insane amount of attention to detail I gave to planning our $10,000 wedding, and literally only a small percentage of that time getting to know the man with whom I was choosing to join my life.

Shortly after we were married, he announced he was buying his own car. On the occasions when he let me borrow it, I found empty Vodka and Old English bottles on the floor behind the driver's seat. He drove quite a distance to work. I asked him about it, but I did not realize it was a problem until he started coming home late intoxicated with what smelled like nicotine on his breath. And then there were police reports and car accidents. I painfully learned that in real life we had very few things in common. While my mother allowed my Dad to roar, I wasn't having it. I said everything I thought I wanted to say. Honestly, we were both in over our heads. We did not know what a marriage looked like without dysfunction. But I forsook everyone to be joined to him. With no sense of self value, I was determined to make it work. I had a lot of heart and no plan.

In 1994, my Granny, my Dad's mother, died and I decided that I would attend the funeral to see my Dad and our relatives. I was nine months pregnant. (This was my second pregnancy so I desired to know if we could have a normal pregnancy. My husband said he was curious too. I stayed sick in bed while my husband stayed out in the streets.) It had been a few years since seeing my Dad. I was hurt because my Dad had not reached out to me since he left the house I grew up in. It was good to see our family. It was especially great to see my Dad although he was hesitant to reach out and hug me. He was not aware that I was married.

We engaged in small talk and I knew my Granny's death was difficult for him. However, I was not prepared for his request to plan his funeral. He told me that his health had deteriorated and he was tired of taking all of the medicine. I asked him not to talk that way.

Two weeks later, my Dad came to the hospital as we were leaving with our newborn son. I invited him over to our apartment. He met my husband and walked through our home as though he was approving it. I later learned that he had called my Mom to make peace with her. I now believe that he had something to share with me also, but I had learned to cope without his earnest attention.

The next call I received, two weeks later, was a request to come to the hospital and identify my Dad's body as the next of kin. This was final. I would never see my Dad alive again. He was the first man I ever loved and there are (still) many questions. As I cleaned his apartment I discovered his struggle and why he may have been unhappy after all those years. At his request, I planned his funeral service. As I reflect on his choices, I made a vow above all else to be true to myself.

In 2002, after ten years of marriage, I told everyone who would listen about my husband leaving us. Inwardly I was crying: "Get him somebody!" I simply did not understand or believe that someone could walk away from the children they had witnessed enter into the world.

On our wedding anniversary, he left a note on the television that he had slept with another woman and was leaving the marriage. We had sons who were three and five years old respectively. I was six months pregnant with our daughter. He had said he wanted a daughter.

I got stuck on the unhappy road of the "why" questions. I remember when he came home early the previous morning and sat at the edge of the bed in deep thought. I remember that familiar distance in the pit of my stomach. I was stuck in a cycle of unanswered questions and assumptions. After the children were born, I became less vocal and more desperate to do whatever I could to make him want to stay. He became violent if I pressed in for more answers. On one occasion, the officer begged me to press charges because he had been to our place before and did not want to find me dead the next time. I did what he said. But he was out of jail within a few days. I was afraid, especially for my children. Things were horrible for a long time and yet I did not have the courage to escape. I was barely functioning.

After he left, I began writing my thoughts in journals. This was my attempt to confront my heart with solid evidence of why this did not work. My anger was increased as I learned about his "happy go lucky" life with his new girlfriend. As soon as I scraped up the money to get a divorce, he married her. I used to believe no one understood him like I did. I attempted to be his protector from the world as he chose time and time again to walk out on me with no real remorse.

The days following this last event, I lay in the bed wanting me and my boys to slip way. I was so tired of the drama and trying to fight for my family alone. I did not want to compete for his attention anymore. People around me cautioned me to keep my thoughts lifted so that my unborn baby girl would not have the effects of my broken heart. The pain was nearly unbearable as I realized that he did not want his family. He did not want me.

What is your story?

Now it is your turn to stop and process your emotions. Acknowledging your feelings about the events that have shaped your life is not accepting defeat. You are taking inventory about where you have been so that you can confront and heal for your fabulous life ahead. This book will help move you forward if you commit to being an overcomer. Will you commit to your well-being?

If you do not value yourself, you teach others not to value you. What do you believe about yourself? Examine your life experiences. I had to be real about the correlation of the painful experiences in my childhood and the dysfunction of my marriage if I was going to become a better parent. Choosing to acknowledge your feelings against the facts of your traumatic experience is a healthy start to the painful events in your life. It is important to pause and process your soul's investment. No one is judging you here. You do not have to rush through this part. Take some deep breaths. Take the time that you need to feel the pain, disappointment, exhaustion and the relief of this moment. Healing does not start until you stop and process what just happened.

CHAPTER TWO

Can I Really Do This Myself?

> For I can do everything through Christ, who gives me strength.
> Philippians 4:13 New Living Translation

Can I restart? Or if not, how do I escape from the crippling residue of life after the trauma? How do I find hope in a hopeless situation? How do I press through the excruciating pain of rejection, broken expectations, anger, fear, regret and receive healing?

Raising children of substance is not for the weak and weary. Ask any parent. It takes absolutely no investment for weeds to grow and choke out a few scattered seeds. And if you plan to do it without regret, you must give everything you have daily and pray for God's grace and mercy on the days you slack off.

Positive parenting after experiencing physical, emotional, and verbal abuse is difficult and sometimes feels nearly impossible. We didn't sign up for this. We wanted the dream. Some parents just ride parenthood out with no desire to learn courage. But if you choose to engage in this phenomenal opportunity, it can change your life forever. With God, all things are possible.

Note from my then self:

My husband was with me for the long labors and delivery of our two boys. How will I manage the labor of our new baby? The thought of taking care of my two toddlers alone finally makes me realize how much my husband does not want to take care of us. He has no concerns about how we will make it after his abrupt departure. Although he has left us before, this time I make the decision to say no more.

I am not sure how me and my children are going to make it. But his access ends here. How did I get here? I am unprepared mentally and financially although the truth was he had not worked in a year. So maybe I can do this. The future of my boys and the baby girl I am carrying are in jeopardy if I cannot figure out how to take care of them by myself.

I never considered abandoning him especially after the children were born. I was committed to patching up and creating other ways to make our marriage work. I was in love with my idea of marriage which was not based in reality. Now that he has left, how much more committed can I be to the children we brought into the world? I prayed and cried out to God to save my marriage. I begged God to give him the desire for his family. God chose rather to deliver us. Now it is time to take courage.

It was mid-September 1999. I wrote a letter to my husband's grandfather. He was a business man. I told him about our situation of not having heat and that we were in danger of losing our place. During my marriage, he would ask about the boys with a concerned look. I did not talk negatively about my husband in a poor attempt to keep my hope alive. When we attach shame to ourselves, we don't seek help. We avoid it.

After he totaled my car and witnessed a young man get fatally shot in front of our apartment building, my husband left us and went back to his grandfather's house. I was devastated that they would allow him to stay there. It did not come to me then that they knew more about his activities than I did.

I humbled myself and eventually reached out to my mother again, with another mouth to feed and no transportation. When I moved back to my mother's house. I felt humiliated because this was the life I chose, and it did not work. It was hard for my family to watch, I imagine … She would call and ask, what was I going to do about the apartment. About the childcare. About the lack of transportation. This was my third stay at her house during my marriage. I knew she was not excited about us returning, but she was glad we were safe.

Now that we were around the corner again as when we were before marriage, my husband's uncle updates me on what my husband is now doing whether I want to hear it or not. It is such a hard truth. If there were any signs of weakness about returning to my husband, I had valid reminders of why that would not be a wise choice. In the valley, there will be crossroads and you must take one-hundred percent responsibility for the road you choose.

Inquisitive by nature, I wanted to understand everything. Sometimes it was too much for my Dad. I asked why. He yelled back, "because I said so!" This is probably why I read so much. Teaching environments excite me and help me understand where I am and where I am going. Scripture says, "mark out a straight path for your feet; stay on the safe path" (Proverbs 4:26 New Living Translation).

After reading the popular book, the *Purpose Driven Life* by Rick Warren, I am fascinated by the truth that we do not have to assume the posture of inadequacy and worthlessness. God actually has a plan for my life (and yours). Years later, as I was trying to make sense of the direction of my life as a single woman and mother, I stumbled across a book by author and coach Valorie Burton called *Listen to Your Life*. Although things did not improve right away, the information in those books and many other books turned my focus on connecting the dots in my own life experiences. Before reading those books, I confess I was "outside minded." By that I mean, I was trying to locate myself in other people and things. I did what others did because I did not know who I was and the value of my gifts. When we are attracted to the gifts in others and do not value the gift inside of ourselves, jealousy comes up rather than admiration.

There was much to learn. Shame was my disposition and it blocked my sight.

When I began studying the Bible, I was confronted with the same verse: Proverbs Chapter 1, verse 22a "How long, ye simple ones, will ye love simplicity?" Wisdom cries in the streets.

The answer is available. Let us locate what we need and change our destination. We can choose to overcome rather than continue in a downward spiral or barely exist.

You can be a parent transforming with strength and dominion.

CHAPTER THREE

Who Am I Now After the Trauma?

> He sent his word, and healed them, and delivered them from their destructions. Psalm 107:20 King James Version

I wish I could tell you that my journey has been clean and pretty. I have been fortunate to receive therapeutic lessons from professionals and preachers alike, but the best lessons on this journey have been by mistakes and meditation. There has been much self-awareness and growth throughout the years. Who knew that what I saw as my deepest pain would turn out to be the force that launched my desire to support other parent leaders.

Parenting allows us to access our experience of childhood twice. God says, I know how you felt as a child. But here is an opportunity to minister to that need so that you can stop the curse of lack and emotional poverty in future generations forever. My heavenly Father says, I now give you, who are broken yet committed, an opportunity to nurture your seed for an abundant harvest.

Isaiah 41:10 KJV is the scripture God gave me as I wrote the lyrics to "My Promise to you."

"Fear thou not; for I am with thee: be not dismayed; for I am thy God: I will strengthen thee; yea, I will help thee; yea, I will uphold thee with the right hand of my righteousness."

We have his promise. He has blessed you and I to bring a child into the world and now we have his promise as we demonstrate stewardship over the gift in our hands.

When everything else seems to fail, who will you trust?

I attempted to move forward on my journey after the trauma. I failed miserably. I was irresponsible to trust that others knew what is best for me and my children.

When we don't take responsibility for our reactions to what happens in our life, it is easier to blame someone else. I continued to serve faithfully as a minister and worship leader during my difficult marriage. I heard God say during fasting and prayer to feed my sheep. I wanted to hide under the pews, but my spiritual leaders at the time encouraged me to keep going. I was honored to serve. My Grandfather served in ministry for over 60 years. He was my inspiration, supporting the needs of people inside and outside of the church. The church leaders emphasized the study of scripture and because I was so hungry for truth, I studied as much as I could.

It felt easier to cope if everything else stayed the same around me as my family life crumbled publicly. My church became the center of my life and my only outlet besides work. I took on an unhealthy approach to what I thought was a secure environment. After all, they knew me best, right? My pastor stood me up at random times and announced to the congregation that my husband left me with three kids. He would add, "… but she's still holding on." People would clap and pity me. This confused me as I fought mentally to rediscover a ray of hope after my world crumbled into fragments of despair. I began to wonder if rejection would be my identity for the remainder of my life.

Those insensitive words were sent to cripple and victimize me and my children, despite the profession of love for us. I confided in my spiritual leader each time my husband left on a binge. He listened on the telephone but responded to the outpouring of my heart on the microphone in the midst of the congregation. "If I was her, I would …" It was hard to hear. I slowly realized that the decision to heal and move forward was mine alone.

It seemed like as time went on, there was an attempt to undermine the authority caused by my ministry assignment within the walls of the congregation in which I served. But as I kept preaching and singing, the transparency about my struggles increased my influence among the people without me noticing it. Whatever good people saw in me was only because God was hiding me in him. And I drew strength from the prayers and encouragement of the people. There was a song I used to sing, "Well, it's the power of God that keeps holding me up and it keeps on holding me up." I did not seek popularity. I just wanted us all free.

My greatest battle to overcome was in my home.

Therefore, the decision to disconnect from other toxic relationships was easier. I decided that I did not want to preach anymore if it would bring more rejection. However, I lacked direction so I stayed on my knees, praying to God. Deep within my soul, I desired a better life for my children that looked very different than where I found myself. I desired more courage.

What crossroads do you face in your story? What tough decisions must you make for the sake of moving your family forward?

Sadly, many parent leaders suffer and are paralyzed by the opinions of family and friends who only know part of our stories and feel like they have a right to broadcast it, along with their commentary. The temptation is to shrink in silence, especially if they are offering money or resources that you and your family need. Remember no one can tell your story better than you.

Among other valuable lessons, I learned that people attempt to restrict you to their own perspectives and limitations. When you allow people to squash the passion in your heart, you minimize the effectiveness of your assignment. The charge of somehow raising two sons and a daughter alone was massive to me. While I appreciated the support, I did not look to the church leadership and congregation to redefine my life as parent leader.

With the activity surrounding my life in my new single parent role, I could finally relax because there was no more unmet expectation for sharing responsibilities. You cannot control the heart of another no matter how much you depend on them. It was a painful truth but once met and understood, things became a whole lot more peaceful. With my children in bed with me, I decided to focus more on praying for the wisdom to take care of my neglected children who fell between the cracks of me doing relationship patchwork and ministry work.

I entered survival mode handling only what was in front of me. My world focused on paying tithes and offering, having enough money to travel to work and church and making sure I had enough formula, pampers and money for the caregiver each week. My children needed me. I was exhausted, but I did not have time to notice that I had lost me along the way. There is a better way. He sent his word and delivered me from destroying myself.

Why is the work of pursuing wholeness so important? The person you were at the start of your relationship is not the person you are today. Imagine applying glue between two sheets of paper. If you attempt to rip those sheets apart, both would be visibly torn with pieces of the other sheet attached. In the same way, it is impossible to be the same after you have joined yourself with another person and have had that ripped asunder.

Do your current decisions display your pain or your promise?

Moving Forward

There was significant healing when I made learning God's Word a priority—not just for sharing it with others but for strengthening me daily. In my marriage I was changed into someone I did not recognize. There was desperation. I settled for less than what my heart wanted. I finally accepted that my life as it had been was unhealthy for me and our children.

Bible reading held a space for one. It was the planting of who I was created to be before the foundation of the world. I was fed on a diet of John, Chapters 14 and 15. I read it repeatedly before bed when my wound was fresh. I did not understand all of it, but it became my salve, my strength.

"Let not your heart be troubled neither let it be afraid … Abide in me as my words abide in you and you can ask anything and it will be done unto you."

Tears rolled down my face.

Soon, I began to seek out abundant living. I desired it more than revenge. Isaiah Chapter 54 is one that speaks out to me time and time again. Not for him or them with evil intentions toward me but for me alone. In my heart, it is no longer a requirement for him to be part of my circle of happiness. I do not have to be consumed with what he is doing. Thinking of him less and myself more, I sincerely desire for my children to live and love freely. During my meditation on the truth of God's holy word, I started seeing myself as an overcomer and not a victim.

I wish above all things that you prosper and be in health, even as your (emotional) soul prospers. This peace I came to know is everything.

Forgiveness

Holding on to painful memories takes excessive energy and steals away precious moments that could be devoted to love and appreciation for a life well lived and healthy connections to those you love. It is harder to hold on to the anger and hostility in anticipation of telling the person how they hurt you. I did not realize the mind-body connection of holding on to deadly emotions. Bitterness of the soul sets in the bones and causes other health problems. In the past, I suffered with debilitating back problems at stressful times.

Forgiveness did not come easy for me. It is a deliberate decision. But I did not know where to start. What do you do when everyone around you seems to be going along with the program but their lives show evidence of misery? The general attitude was just "act" right. Newsflash somebody! When you are in pain, everything hurts. You act wrong because your heart is troubled. Just when I think I have dealt with one area, something else appears. Jesus can you get to the root of this and heal my heart? Can you heal my emotions? Yes, He says, "Come to me, all of you who are weary and carry heavy burdens, and I will give you rest. Take my yoke upon you. Let me teach you, because I am humble and gentle at heart, and you will find rest for your souls. For my yoke is easy to bear, and the burden I give you is light." Matthew 11:28-30 NLT

Some families believe it is not right to "air the dirty laundry" and otherwise attempt to hum it away, pat it away, or fan it away. These are also families that carry disease from generation to generation. Forgiving my parents for what I felt I did not receive as a child was easier when I consider their perspective and childhood experiences. I believe they love me as much as they are able. I honor them and I am grateful for their efforts especially now that I am a parent. There are many parents who remain emotionally unavailable to their child because of unresolved issues.

Over the years during our conversations, I asked for forgiveness for words spoken out of pain to my former husband. I decided I wanted God's favor with me and the children more than I want to remain stuck in anger. Please note that this is different than offering access to those emotional places that were once vulnerable. Scripture says "Guard your heart above all else, for it determines the course of your life." Proverb 4:23.

As my children grow older, I make attempts to harness a relationship with their paternal grandmother to keep the children connected to their family. She is a blessing to us. Through her, their father is invited to activities, award ceremonies and the graduations of the children. He yells the loudest, but there is no change with his level of care or concern. Nonetheless, the children are encouraged. As time goes on, I accept that he may never get the courage to confront his life decisions.

What if you never get an apology?

If you allow one toxic relationship, it is almost a given that there are other toxic relationships in your life. I struggle with letting go of the pattern of toxic relationships and friendships that kept me stuck in pity and self-defeating cycles until I learned that it is also a form of self-sabotage. Toxicity numbs your senses. We lay down when we should stand tall.

I thought because I had committed my marriage to God, I was locked in forever, despite the emotional and physical abuse. I learned that some situations we get ourselves in are not God's will. God reminds me of the free will given to every man. I am not in control of my ex-husband's will. Every person must answer to Almighty God for themselves. In addition, everyone is given the same opportunity to confront past mistakes and to receive grace to start over.

I also nearly drown in guilt that yields to manipulation. My mother told me not to get married and I did it anyway and now I have children. I felt like I deserved the distant treatment or memory recall she measures out when I call her for help. Therefore, I am tempted to live the remainder of my life fulfilling her desires just so she can finally be pleased with me as I take all sorts of detours to find my life. She is not particularly interested in babysitting the children, but she does. She yells, "feed your kids!" or calls me at work to ask when I am coming home.

But Mom was with me when I had my daughter, as well as my other children. She took me to the doctor that morning. We walked the mall until we went to the hospital. I asked the nurses to let me use the bathroom before they checked me. They insisted on checking me first. When they did, they saw the baby's head! I delivered my daughter within 20 minutes. The long labor I was so afraid of took place very quickly. I am grateful for answered prayer.

While I love my family, and appreciate everything they did to help us, I realize giving up my apartment did not put me in a better place because of the unresolved issues of my father's house. And now in their sight, me and my children are needy rather than in need of "temporary" help. I am working hard not to be a burden or an interruption in the lives of others. Each person has a right to decide how they move forward if at all. If I was going to change their perception, I had to work toward independence. My new car became my prayer room. I cried out hard to God for healing and more wisdom. "Lord, make me better and not bitter."

In time as I confronted the truth, I learned the necessary act of forgiving myself. This is a difficult task when there are those around you constantly reminding you of your shortcomings. Faith the size of a mustard seed requires an overcomer's mentality. I did not notice exactly when there were no more tears on my pillow. But I started to notice my excitement for the new day and the promise of hope for tomorrow. My outside world did not change right away, but my desires for restoration were stronger. Forgiving yourself means choosing what feeds and nurtures your soul.

If you are going to survive this moment and be able to speak into the lives of your future, you must leave dead things in the graveyard. Wherever you find yourself today, God is able to bring clarity and peace to your heart so that you can fully walk in your parental assignment.

CHAPTER FOUR

Spiritual Renewal

> "Don't copy the behavior and customs of this world, but let God transform you into a new person by changing the way you think. Then you will learn to know God's will for you, which is good and pleasing and perfect." Romans 12:2 New Living Translation

Is your place of worship an atmosphere helpful for healing and restoration? If not, you are in the wrong place. Are you submitted to a leader who speaks faith into your life regularly? Sometimes you have to believe someone else's *positive* view of you until you are strong enough to believe in yourself. Just ensure they have your best interests at heart. Some people only thrive when we are crippled, as they use our pain for a crutch.

Albert Einstein says, "We can't solve problems by using the same kind of thinking we used when we created them." And while it is easy to pick up a book or watch a video on the subjects, meditation and affirmations without belief do not work. Bodily exercise profits very little if we fail to acknowledge the attacks on our soul. If it was that easy, we would all be free from the horrible, long-term effects of trauma. Our world would be a much safer place for our children.

Before moving on to a new place of worship, I attempted to make peace with my spiritual leader about us moving forward. As a ministry leader, I wanted to thank him for the opportunity to serve and learn. I knew the general assumption was that people would stay there until they died. In fact, people said that often. My ears would ring. I certainly didn't have any plans on dying right away. He responded that once we leave, he was no longer required to pray for us. While I was not prepared to hear such an abrupt closure, his reaction spoke again to the toxic connections that I allowed to invade my life.

When we feel we are not enough, we tend to make agreements that may not necessarily serve us as we expand. I was now leader of my family. By prayer and fasting, I was overcoming major hurdles. I learned many things, but my soul was thirsty for more. I also craved the plan of God to be revealed for my family. I simply could not give up.

How many people stay at spiritual places they have outgrown because of relationships alone? They have allowed distractions to leave their families in the mud. It had been eight years. Eight is the number of new beginnings.

My new place of worship is refreshing. Hearing God's word strengthens and empowers me to minister to the souls of my children and others I encounter who are suffering from the effects of trauma. During our time there, God was training and building my confidence in how he speaks to me personally. He speaks audibly, by impression, in pictures and dreams … "Ask, and it shall be given you; seek, and you shall find; knock, and the door shall be open unto you." Matthew 7:7 It is your duty to quiet your life so you can hear. If we don't know, we dismiss it and miss opportunities that reveal to us the best of God in the next season.

The fellowship of people who have similar values and beliefs as you is a great source of encouragement. A church family can sometimes be closer to you than your birth family. However, it should not be the agenda of a church environment to sabotage your family bond. When I receive compliments about the pleasant demeanor of my children, it lets me know that I am healing internally. At random times, people would bless my children with gifts or say something meaningful to them. It was important to me that they were being ministered to also as they dealt with life without the other parent. The right church community strengthens you when you and your family need it most.

When my children were younger, our church would have all night Friday prayer twice a month. Often, they were the only children there. They would be asleep on the pews. I would be sitting or kneeling pouring out my fears and concerns about this great responsibility. I realized that the spirit of God in me is perfect, but my soul needs salvation. As I grew in my knowledge of the Lord Jesus Christ, I leaned less on the wisdom of men and more on the wisdom of God. I somehow knew that whatever God had planned for me, he had good planned for my children also. This is important because when we think we are not enough, we think there are not enough resources for our family. Parent leader, there is enough. So, I make decrees based on scripture about our lives as we move forward.

After exactly eight years, God led me to an environment of faith through a prayer class in which I enrolled. I had no immediate plans to change my place of worship as I had completed a nine-month class and received my assignment to teach the toddlers in Sunday School. I was an active member of the choir. It also meant that I would have to drive forty minutes to the other side of town. But it was in alignment with what I needed to receive blessing and favor for my household.

After our transition, my son received his healing after a 10-year health battle, completed trade school and received gainful employment. My other son received favor to run a man's business before he turned 19 while earning his first degree. My daughter chose to serve at church which allowed her the right amount of skills to obtain her first job and was eventually offered a four-year merit college scholarship. I recorded four songs and trained to finish marathons to improve my health and endurance. My faith decrees for my children are being fulfilled by the grace of God. When we obey the moves of God, God moves on our behalf.

Man is triune. This means that man is spirit that has a soul and lives in a body. Our body decays daily but our spirit never dies. God is spirit. We live out of our soul … our mind (our thoughts), will (our decisions), intellect (our reasoning), emotions and imagination (creative scenarios). If we want to know about our life as it is, we should consult above all else the One who created us. If we choose, our spirit can connect to the infinite wisdom of God through his son, Jesus. He is the only true way. He knows us perfectly. But our free will allows us to give ourselves to whomever we choose. Regardless of what we've been through though, if we allow him to, Jesus can bring healing to our soul.

We do not have to remain in the same state of mind that allows us to be mistreated by others. Your healing is a part of your success equation. If not, the negative cycle continues for the next generation. Scripture says for all who are led by the Spirit of God are sons of God. Sons speaks of heritage not gender. Is personal ministry available at your place of worship? Don't retreat. Press in. Are you able to schedule time for godly counsel about the next steps in your life? No one but you can decide what is best for you; however, it is great to learn about other avenues of expression, such as family therapy or coaching. Is there a youth ministry that will allow your child to build positive peer relationships? If you decide to attend another church like we did, your genuine friendships will remain and support you.

Sometimes your current environment, which includes family and friends, does not support your desire for freedom from the damage of your past. Some people say, "I remember when you …" if they think you are getting away from your past too quickly. You can acknowledge it but inform them that it is no longer your emotional location. You have moved on. Whether your current environment accepts your growth or not, growth is a part of your existence. Every living thing is able to grow.

Many parents purchase homes in gated communities or buy a cabinet of firearms to protect their family from danger. We must also ensure we protect our children from spiritual molestation. Had I continued my membership at the same church community, my children and I would operate from a victim's mentality. I decided that as parent leader, I alone am responsible for placing my family in an atmosphere that enlarges us spiritually.

As a leader, you are also responsible for protecting your child's emotions. Attacks that come against their purpose are real. The plan of destruction for your family is often an undercover operation, filled with dark and blurry pathways. The nightmares your child experience now will continue to follow and possibly overtake him in his lifetime if you don't battle on behalf of his purpose. A parent should be ready to discern and war on behalf of your child's present and future. This involves maintaining a lifestyle that is clear and open to receive knowledge and understanding by the spirit of Almighty God for you and your child. Sometimes I am led to pray and later hear that there was a near-miss experience. This reminds me of how aggressive the parents are in my daughter's honors classes. While I am grateful she is doing well, some parents put a demand on the teacher about what they expect for their child. Put a demand on your child's wholeness. Go all out!

If you want to receive your assignment as a skilled warrior on behalf of your child, your spiritual renewal must be birthed in prayer. This is not a monologue, but a dialogue that involves listening and talking, making requests and giving thanks. An appointment with your Creator is best for parents who have experienced trauma. Regular prayer time imparts patience to listen to God's direction. You can provide an open environment that allows your children to express themselves fully without judgment or abandonment. Sometimes what you hear may hurt you deeply or cause you anxiety, but you can pour out your heart to God. You are not alone. His presence is a sustaining power that causes you to see beyond the circumstance. He is faithful to hear our deepest cry.

CHAPTER FIVE

The Importance of Language

> Pleasant words are as an honeycomb, sweet to the soul, and health to the bones. Proverbs 16:24 King James Version

We, as parents, can speak health to our children when we work on ourselves. Your child looks in your eyes and asks, "Who am I in this world?" She watches how well you handle life to learn about herself. The tongue of a parent is a powerful force that resonates in the ear of a child for his entire lifetime.

Most of us realize the words we speak have much power. So, what are you saying to yourself? Even after embracing a more positive and supportive environment, I noticed that I said horrible things to myself when I made mistakes. I hated myself for what I allowed to come into my life. How could I allow someone to be so cruel to me? It did not occur to me that I was repeating what I heard my father say to me as a little girl. He was very harsh with his words. There were no conversations, just commands. He made me tremble inside and out. He was unwavering in his authoritarian parenting style that sought to bend my will rather than understand me.

Unfortunately, timidity became my comfort zone. He would tuck my recognition and award certificates tightly under his arm and put them in his picture album. He instructed me not to touch them. After all, he was an educator. Many people admired him. He was a giant in my eyes. Whatever remarks or compliments I received from others, none was greater than the words I received from my Dad. My husband's actions only confirmed my own self neglect. Up until the note I received that night, he did not admit his wrong, only mine. So, I personalized the events inside our marriage to mean that I was defective.

My mother's silence was eloquent. She did not protect me or calm my fears behind the silver gate that surrounded our house. She may have been scared too or preoccupied as I was with my young children during my marriage. Whatever the case may be, her years of staying with my Dad made it seem like she consented to his treatment of us. Despite needing protection as a child, I felt that I somehow needed to protect her. I worried and had nightmares about her death and would often cry myself to sleep. There were no words of comfort and no prayer offered to calm my fears.

After entering high school, I became fond of others with strong opinions who believed in justice. My Dad felt like he could no longer manipulate me with fear. He said, "I was getting out of hand." He turned me over to my mother and she became active in asking me about my whereabouts after school. She seemed to have the perfect disposition and was greatly disappointed in my wayward choices. In my teen years, she often commented that she never spoke to her mother the way I spoke to her. The guilt I felt in those moments was tremendous. However, the turmoil remained unaddressed.

As a child with limited knowledge, I was angry about why she wasn't curious enough to ask us more questions when she came back from work, or why she chose not to seek help. She would say to me, "You need to talk to someone. You have a problem!" And although she divorced my father, she placed me back into suffocating church environments that did not address my wounds and bring us closer as a family. She got on the organ and played right through it. It seemed like she just replaced my father with overbearing spiritual leaders who she aimed to please. It was hard hearing people disrespect her or overlook her ability because she lacked confidence in herself. In the past, I have exchanged words with others in defense of her, only to be reprimanded by her.

As my children grow older, I learned to find common ground with my mother despite her dismissive stance to the events of my childhood. I do ask random questions to see if she has opened up. I have left her many days holding back tears. It is a work in progress for me because of my curiosity to understand myself. I feel like some of that is tied to understanding her. She is loyal to what she loves and does not like conflict of any kind. So, to her, my strong character comes off as troublesome. I decided that her (sometimes) lack of interest no longer factors into what is best for me and my family.

It seemed she believed I should abandon *whatever it is that I do* to comply with her requests immediately because she is my parent. I felt indebted to her for her gifts and often did things I communicated I was not interested in doing only to make her happy. I chose so-called peace. But the truth is, I cannot repay her for everything that she has done for us. Also, we cannot make anyone else happy. That's their job.

It is difficult to take courage and bid for something I want because of her loud silence. I am not sure if she knows that I struggle with anxiety and confidence too … even if I forge ahead and it just happens to turn out great. I have learned to share good news at the time of celebration, rather than be pre-sabotaged by her doubts and fear.

I accept that we have different perspectives and while I respect my mother's choices, I also respect my own. This has improved our relationship so much because I learned that she does not have to change for my transformation to take place. We have great conversations and she has given me beautiful cards that express how proud she is of me. She often extends herself more than others. She is kind and very generous to us and those around her. I cherish the growth in our relationship. I love her so much.

What language do you hear from your most important relationships? What words are you repeating? What words resound in your ear so loudly that it paralyzes you or moves you forward?

Just a few years ago, I was asked to help organize an injured executive in her office. She was brilliant. She was a recognized influential leader in her industry with top awards on the shelf. However, when she made a mistake, she did not immediately move to find a solution. She continued to ask herself, "Why did I do that?" When she did not like the work product of others, rather than tailor her words carefully to keep the person's ego intact, she let harsh words fly out of her mouth. While going through documents on her desk, I noticed words on a thick document written in red ink, "What were you thinking when you wrote this???" At times she would look at me and ask, why are you so nice to me?

Her secretary was mentally and physically getting worse. The executive failed to acknowledge the inability of her assistant to no longer perform her duties as anything she had caused. She shared with me that she believed her assistant simply takes the wrong medication. She did not attach the lack of comradery among her peers or the high turnover rate of her staff to any behavioral deficits of her own. She simply removed herself from the equation. The staff on her floor ask me in the hallways how am I able to work with her. I smile and say to myself, "Thanks Dad." As a way to show her appreciation for my work there, her secretary purchased gift cards for me and insisted that I take them. Not too long after my time with them, she gained strength to resign after many years.

A group leader I assisted stayed in an intense state most days. He would bite his nails down to his nail beds. When he gave me directions, he would pull his shirt from his neck to readjust. I figured out he wasn't angry. He was just extremely intoxicated by chasing money deals. He "lived" to win. I wondered many days how he treated his wife and children, hoping he was a lot more relaxed at home. I later learned that he had a massive heart attack at age 52, the same age as my Dad.

The irony of all of this is the spoken and unspoken language of my childhood affected and enhanced my ability to be rewarded in the marketplace. The plan and purposes of God, despite our human efforts or lack thereof, continues to be sure. For over twenty years, when God directed my path to downtown Chicago, my career has allowed me to serve and provide administrative support to brilliant and successful parent leaders of organizations and departments in various industries within corporate sectors.

As I assist busy executives, I have been the connection between the leader and his superiors, the leader and his staff and the leader and his family. As an adult, this experience is both exhilarating and challenging. I pray for my own efforts because it is fast paced and there is little room for error. But because of my background, I am sensitive to the person separate from their leadership role, as I prepare documents and presentations, plan meetings, distribute reports and even book his favorite seat for his airline reservation.

I see the fear masked under the corporate cool as they win

at the office and struggle at home. I see the discouragement after working so hard on a deal as he returns to his office, and the temptation to isolate himself as I leave him sitting in his office as the cleaning crew appears for their shift. To remind him of things that make his heart smile, I bring up his children. The countenance on his face changes to one of pure joy. He releases that stiff competitive energy and becomes relaxed as he mentions some great accomplishment that he may have heard about through his spouse or just before bed as he makes it home in time to tuck in his child. Leaders Wellness Suite was created to support the busy parent leader.

Parenting and Guilt

We as parents feel the guilt as we explain yet another time we are not able to make it home for dinner. After apologizing so much, some just stop communicating. The unspoken language is: "Accept it. It is what it is." I have had executives I support tell me to contact them at their vacation spot with their families——or they call in from vacation and attend meetings via conference call for hours. We chop it up in social settings about where our children go to school, but we don't really know much more than that. We leave our responsibility in the hands of our spouse. They have to be the encourager and disciplinarian. "It is for a noble cause," you say. But we give in to societal pressures of maintaining our jobs, promotions, relationships or social high life at the expense of our children. The words we speak have much power.

"Just go outside and play."
"Do not call me at work."

One parent told me she does not want to know what her sons do when they are out of her presence. Ignorance does not cancel our responsibility.

What do we say when we are too busy to recognize when our child has entered a new developmental stage? I had an opportunity to work in a middle school to help my son recover from his injury. Not only did I learn about special education services that are made available to help children with special needs, I learned to serve children as a library aide. Children are brilliant in the way they pick up social cues. These children in their early adolescence asked their teachers to come to the library to get a book, but often just wanted to talk to me. Their pure thoughts and candid words made me sit up and take notice. One student told me she wanted to put a curse on her mother because she refuses to buy her the gym shoes she wants. Does her mother know she is attracted to Black Magic? Another student shows me scars on her arms from her foster parent. My desk was between the offices of the school psychologist and the social worker so when parents did not show up for meetings regarding the performance or behavior of their child, I saw that too. Behavioral problems sometimes develop from the confusion of what the child sees in his home or his reaction to it. I am not trained in child psychology. I only testify to my own experiences and what my eyes witnessed for four years.

Safety in and outside of the home is crucial for a child to continue a normal pattern of growth. Our children are not created to live in disorder. In Jewish tradition, a father places his hand on top of his son's head and prays a blessing over him. Catholics baptize their young child. Christian parents dedicate their child to the Lord. Although my grandparents lived in Michigan, three hundred miles away, I am blessed to have had their prayer support for as long as I have been alive. When we would arrive to visit, my grandfather would hug us tightly and stop and pray a blessing over us. When I would share a dilemma with him, he had great stories but most times, he would just pray a blessing. And then just before hitting the highway to return home, he would pray a blessing over us and give me and my little brothers some cash. As he got older and was ready to get off the phone, in the middle of my sentence he would start praying down blessings. Of course, he knew how strict my Dad was in his religious beliefs, but I don't know whether he knew much more than that about our household. I cherish the language in this memory. Could his prayer be the reason I am here today? Children who have been in traumatic situations should be handled with extended care, first by the parent and then by others.

Your Child Needs Your Best

There is a news story that captured my attention where two brothers entered into a restaurant where their mother worked. Soon after, a man with a gun came into the restaurant and shot the two customers who were standing in the restaurant. The two brothers ran out of the restaurant. The shooter ran out behind them. More gunfire erupted. The newspaper says that "the mother knew that her sons had just ran out." Both of her sons were laying on the ground for hours covered with white sheets while the police investigated their murders.

My heart drops as I think about the thoughts of that mother who was unable to protect her sons. I pray for every parent who has lost a child. How much of our youth's blood cry out from our streets? There are also young people dying of drug overdoses in the suburbs. They have nice cars and beautiful houses but are unaware of their irreplaceable value to parents who are intoxicated by status, greed and competition. This world system of industry is designed to entice you to chase the wind for temporary pleasure at such a great expense.

Because of the chaos of this world, and the fact that tomorrow is not promised, I think about my children living without me some day. For all ostensible purposes, they have already lost their other parent so I'm it. I have turned down opportunities in my life because every opportunity is not a good opportunity for me if it conflicts with my commitment to my young children.

What does parent success look like to you? Set the expectation. If you constantly complain about your job, but choose to stay, your child may not think much about finding work he enjoys. If education is not your thing, don't expect your child to get a Ph.D. While you cannot give what you do not have, choose to encourage your child to do well in the areas aligned with their purpose, not yours. Choose to model in word and deed.

Choose to pour your "first fruits" into your children and then share the remainder with the world. Choose to work toward a stable environment after trauma, with care to surround your children with trustworthy mentors who will encourage them and build them up. Some parents have extended family support. Grandparents can play a key role in the lives of our children. Some aunts and uncles are like second parents.

Who are you allowing to speak into your future?

Motivational speaker, Jim Rohn stated, we become like the five people we hang out with the most. Do your close family and friends speak of possibilities or struggle? Do they stretch you to consider new perspectives? How do we avoid choosing habits and activities that neither empower us or our children? Who do you share your dreams with?

As a leader, I encourage you to see beyond your current circumstances. Relationships that do not challenge us to seek a higher place emotionally for ourselves and the world in which we live do us a disservice. In addition, wrong associations can hinder your progress to wholeness. Do not allow anyone (especially yourself) to keep you in victim pity status at any time. You cannot afford to raise children who see themselves as victims or inferior. Guard your heart and your mind continually. Your child deserves every opportunity to live whole without the limitations placed on him by your choices and negative experiences. Serve your experiences only as references as you consider your child's personality and judgment. Your guidance is imperative. But the only way it will be purposeful, passionate and edifying is if you are fully invested in moving forward.

CHAPTER SIX

Embrace Your Authority

> Children are a gift from the LORD; they are a reward from him. Children born to a young man are like arrows in a warrior's hands. Psalm 127:3-4 New Living Translation

You are your child's first teacher and your imprints are for life. We cannot lead in fear and insecurity and expect to raise resilient children. Nor can we expect others to take our place.

According to *Psychology Today*, researchers identified three common parental styles. Authoritarian style demands obedience and operates in the idea that in order to maintain discipline, it is necessary to control all areas of the child's behavior as if to break their will. The second style is permissive which is very loving yet provides few guidelines and rules. Lastly, authoritative parenting involves high expectations while providing children with the resources and support they need to succeed. There are two parental styles that are possibly found more in traumatic situations. The neglectful parent style does not respond to a child's needs. The indifferent, uninvolved parent makes few or no demands and is emotionally indifferent, dismissive or completely absent.

Can you identify the parenting style of your parents? Your parenting style? The parenting style of the other parent? How do we bridge the gap when there has been trauma?

Parenting does not require perfection. It does, however, require everything else you are. Your influence works better with openness, patience and understanding. You are expected to teach forgiveness by asking for forgiveness. You are expected to share and model. "Do as I say" is not as loud as "do as I do."

My own limitations are challenged as my children show interest in areas unfamiliar to me. If you are raising more than one child like I am, you discover that each child is unique in the way he relates to his surroundings and the world. As a parent, children are the main entree. Every other area in life are the side dishes until your children reach the age of accountability.

In addition, I realize that because of my abusive background, my views may be distorted at times. I learn to yield and trust God rather than "lean unto my own understanding." At times I fail, but then I rely on their viewpoint and judgment. This allows me another chance to hear my child exercise his ability to think.

Settle in as a parent leader. What are some of the words you use when you are pleased? Focus on your present assignment as you pour fresh soil for the seeds of an abundant harvest. Your child is a gift. This includes spending more physical time with each other. Decide to be your child's number one cheerleader. I add their events to my calendar so I can encourage them ahead of the event. I also get the word out about their achievements on social media so my children know that even with all my "busyness," they are on my radar. They say, "Mom, why do you post our business?" I say, "How would you know if you did not look?"

This is also a great way to let the other parent and family members know that the children are well if they are not directly involved. It was my intention to include their father's family in our events until they were older to establish their own connection. I cannot erase the fact that the other parent may not choose to be in my child's life as much as we would like. I cannot shield my child from thinking about it. But I can actively listen to their concerns and celebrate their accomplishments. As they get older, our children may not appreciate our presence as much. But in the end, it will serve them well to know they have your attention should they need it. My children text, call and come into my bedroom to tell me what's on their mind. I cherish it so much. Even if I do not agree, I know I can serve them by providing options and praying that they make the best decision.

We can commit to making our child's growth a priority as well as our own. Raising them as victims robs them of their potential. Our painful past does not have to be their fortunate future. As a warrior appointed by God himself, point your child as arrows to affect your house, your community and the world. Let's make so much noise about the positive moments until it feels so good they do it again and again. Goal setting and positive reinforcement has helped each of my children move forward. I often receive character compliments from teachers and other parents who know my children in our community. Business leaders hire and trust these children with keys to their businesses. I am grateful that these leaders see, support and invest time in the potential of my children. The proof of wisdom is results.

Caregivers

Finding a caregiver is a big deal for parents after trauma. There are many things to consider besides the money, including transportation, time, location and environment. It may be cheaper and more convenient for your family members to look after your children, but will they care for them? Many parents do not consider the experience and temperament of the caregiver. Awful things happen to children when they are left in the care of people who do not have their best interests at heart, especially after trauma.

When my husband left abruptly, in my attempt to piece together my life, I asked Mrs. Bea, who attended church with us, if she would care for my sons at her home during the day just until I could figure out what to do. She agreed. Her home was close to the train station and, more importantly, she genuinely loves my children to life. And they clearly love her because after spending all day with her, they were not ready to leave when I returned! Indeed, after work, I did not immediately leave either. It was a pleasure to spend time with the angel who helped to make a difficult time easier. It is a blessing to have an objective voice who you trust to speak life into your child's emotions on a daily basis. Mrs. Bea began caring for other children also.

There are times when I have had to call our caregiver and ask her to care for the children longer in order to complete tasks at work. She and her daughters accommodated me most times. When I called my mother, she would go get the boys but because she works third shift, it put more pressure on me to hurry and complete my work so that she could at least take a nap before rushing off to work. After having my daughter, Mrs. Bea's home is where my daughter's father first met her. Six months after the birth of our daughter, when my boss asked me to accompany the team to Cancun Mexico for their weekend conference, Mrs. Bea agreed to care for the children. It was a much-needed getaway, at the finest accommodations. I took it to mean that God was enlarging my borders to receive greater insight. I thank Mrs. Bea often even after so many years, but I do not think I can ever repay her for what she means to my family.

Know that the person caring for your child is imparting values and beliefs to your child and that they gain their trust. It is imperative that you be a language cop to what others say during the time you are transitioning to wholeness. I am sure my children had lots to say about the conversations I had with their father when they got to Ms. Bea's house. She loved us just the same.

Some people ask questions or have negative comments about the other parent in front of your child without considering that your child may be applying their comments to himself. They speak to let you know they support you, but you should let them know that it does not support your child.

School

Education was important to my parents and it is important to me. I regret that I did not continue my education because I would have avoided all of the night classes while raising a family. When my children were ready for elementary school, I wanted to put them in private school, but I could not afford it. I learned about the charter school lottery system. The day the newly built school opened, I get a letter to say that they were accepted. It was quite a distance. Fortunately, I was blessed to have the children's grandparents to drop them off.

Schools are run by humans with emotions. Studies show that positive attachments with adults increase self-worth, self-esteem and security. While parents are highly sensitive about how their children are treated at school, choose to forge partnerships with the people who are paid to care for your child. You cannot pay people enough to care. However, you can serve them kindness in exchange for genuine concern for your child. What are you willing to do to ensure your child receives a quality education? Even if it surpasses your knowledge, are you willing to sacrifice to help your child advance in school? When we bully teachers and principals, it may get your child a higher grade or a part in the school play, but does it serve your ability to build and sustain a relationship that will help your child achieve academic success?

Sometimes in our attempt to advocate for our child, we do them a disservice. Often, we do not consider that they have to live with the consequences of our actions. I learned about the weightiness of sacrifice from my son who decided to join the volleyball team in his freshman year. Despite the many questions about why he was not interested in basketball because of his height (and other stereotypes), he got along with his teammates and went to their houses for the team dinners. It seemed the other moms and dads on his volleyball team all got along quite well. They were cordial , but it was clear they were not looking for any new besties. My son asked that when I attended games, I would try harder to reach out to them. He did not know that one of the heavily involved parents rode the same train into the city with me. She saw me because I saw her, but she avoided eye contact. While the team grew closer, the parents did not want their world changed. We chose not to be offended by reason of a greater focus. This stance proves to be a shield as we move forward. For four years, I left work to serve on the concession stands, attended most games and attempted to stay neutral so he could participate in something he enjoyed.

In grade school, it may be helpful to talk to the teacher or principal so that they can support your child as he adjusts to the changes in the household. Some parents are not open to discussing personal matters with school personnel and instruct their child to do the same, missing any opportunity to work through challenges at school and at home. Some parents never acknowledge the child's emotions because they are afraid to acknowledge their own. So, your child goes out into the world confused about how he feels about himself and the people who love him. This leaves him prey for wrong associations, depression, substance abuse and more. I learned courage on behalf of my children because I am aware of what the statistics report about children in single parent households. Statistically, they are more likely to abuse drugs, have babies out of wedlock, become involved in crime, run away and commit suicide.

Choosing schools with an abundance of activities appealed to my children's curiosity and creativity. It built their confidence in a new environment as it gave them a chance to participate in teams, gain friendships and enjoy healthy competition. They became champions because of what interest them. It was a healthy distraction and I have had many occasions to cheer them on or take pictures with them holding their awards.

If a child acts out at home or at school, he may not feel heard. Find a good time to talk to your child in a relaxed environment. Seek help. Schedule a meeting with the teacher. In addition, your child may receive a referral to be tested for a learning disability simply because it is difficult to unravel the complex events that come with broken families. If this is the case, work with the school to make things easier for your child. An Individual Education Plan (IEP) is a legal document that is developed for each child who attends public school and require accommodations.

Be intentional about gaining information and coming to

the aid of your child.. In 2006, my son was assaulted and suffered an injury that caused a seizure and left him with stroke-like symptoms including a paralyzed arm and right-sided weakness. All of my children were born healthy and I had worked from a very early age, but when this incident happened, I was in between jobs. When I called my mother as I leaned over my son's body, she yelled on the phone, "Why did you leave our church?" A burst of tears rolled down my cheeks because she was unable to be in this awful moment with us. As parent leader, when you do not properly stop and process your own emotions, you are emotionally unavailable for your child. I called my son's other grandparents and they came right away. It was a very difficult season for me and the children. It was the hardest thing I ever had to endure as a parent. My son asked repeatedly, "Mom, what are you going to do?" I really didn't know, but there is a strength that comes from above that carries us in our weakest hour.

My son did not receive a diagnosis right away. The emergency medicine physician instructed me to put him back in school and he would be fine in a few days. That was not the case. His condition became more perplexing. There were so many unanswered questions to the extent that the hospital became a weekly field trip. At one point, he had to be homeschooled. The teacher agreed to come to our home to teach him for a few hours so that he could pass his grade. I researched local support groups, associations on the city and state level and other hospital specialists to get information on his injury. As my son got older and we thought that his health challenges were resolved, he began receiving detentions and reports for his behavior. Have you ever had to go to school and hear about your child's behavior and you had no explanation? More research was needed.

My full-time focus was finding information. I found favor with skilled professionals with advanced degrees to help me provide letters and written physician referrals. We went into the school and asked for tests to be ordered so that he could receive educational support by law. I was quite uncomfortable because I knew nothing about the world of special education. Remember, I went to private school. I had so many meetings where I saw both parents waiting and I was by myself. I walked out of meetings with my requests granted on behalf of my son and several school educators only by God's grace. I was nervous but "prayed up." One day, the meeting facilitator told my son that he is blessed to have a mother who is willing to speak up on his behalf. Warrior parent leader, everything you need to lead your child to wholeness is already in you.

After one school meeting, I decided to go see a movie in the middle of the day to unwind. On a normal weekday, I would have been at work because by this time I worked at the school to be available to my son. When I arrived at the snack counter, I saw my children's father with a young lady from our former church, just as content as he wanted to be. I smiled and kept it moving. Inside, it crushed me that he was not involved in the fight. Yes, fighting for your child's well-being is a war.

Most of my direction came as I was praying for God to

keep my heart and mind. Walking the floor at night decreeing healing and wholeness while my son was in the hospital (again), all I had was my faith. I visited the church of the teacher who came to our home and her pastor said that my son would be all right. I asked God to help my unbelief as I saw my son depressed, extremely angry and withdrawn. There were people praying with me in the distance, but it was still a lonely place.

Focusing on getting my child well, I was out of balance. My other children felt neglected. We went to family counseling so they could express their frustrations and feel heard. The truth was tough to take but it was good for us. When a tragedy happens in a family, everyone in the household is affected. I was sad to hear my son share the awful things he remembered from the marriage. God saved our lives when he did not answer my prayers for marriage reconciliation. It is difficult to confront the hard stuff but we started working through it. It caused me to make tough decisions that would help my son have a promising future. I came to the realization that I needed help outside of myself if I was going to help my family. Have you ever been so overwhelmed that you know you need more help? I humbled myself. Men and women appeared like angels ready to help us. In addition to addressing our pain as a family, we were able to get the necessary approvals to get my son the medical attention he needed. Only a mighty God got us through it.

Discipline

> Discipline your children, and they will give you peace of mind and will make your heart glad. Proverb 29:17 New Living Translation

Children and routines are not a perfect science, but healthy boundaries are safe. Discipline is necessary to teach, guide and protect from dangers of all sorts. After trauma, it can be difficult to administer punishment or rules with consequences that are understood properly. Discipline should be handled with a higher level of sensitivity. The core of this must be love and patience. In a 2014 New York Times article about corporal punishment within the African American community, Michael Eric Dyson distinguishes the term discipline which comes from the Latin word "discipuli" which connotes disciple from punishment which comes from the Greek "poine" and Latin "poena" which means revenge, from which comes the words "pain" and "penalty." If a child interprets your correction to be out of how you feel about yourself, he may interpret it to be more about him than the misdeed.

My Dad believed children should be seen and not heard. But God gave our children eyes and ears too. My Mother allowed us to say a little more as she was more passive in her approach. With that said, if someone at church or school reported on my conduct, my parents never asked me anything before punishing me on site. If something foul happened to me, I did not find refuge in my parents. I suffered in silence for fear I would be blamed anyway. I desire to know the thoughts of my children and then we will discuss actions later. Scripture says get wisdom and in all your getting, get an understanding.

Some parents, like my father, say damaging words mixed with strong emotion followed by a hit. After returning to my Mother's house, I was very protective of my boys being spanked because of what they experienced in our home under the care of their father. My three-year-old had a broken arm at two months. My five-year-old suffered a gash at the top of his head. As I adjusted to the single parent life, out of my anger, exhaustion and overwhelm, I also discovered that I handled my sons in the wrong attitude. It hurt me so bad because while I knew discipline was needed, I did not want them to misinterpret it because I was fragmented. I eventually abandoned spanking to find other ways to discipline my children i.e. talking about consequences, limiting television privileges or assigning a repetitive writing exercise. Sometimes I would wait and trust the loud silence when they requested a treat from me. More often, after trauma, our emotional display of love is less than the intense emotion of correcting our child for undesirable behavior. Pause and think about it. When we know better, we do better.

Sometimes parents pity their children and choose to take a low control stance out of guilt because they work long hours and feel they cannot control what they do when they are not present. This may be why some children are in the streets past the city curfew or spend hours with the wrong crowd with no accountability. I think it is important that parents set the expectation so that the children can have a standard to return to. Teen years are challenging for parents as children begin to explore other influences and develop a level of independence. Some comply and others are curious about what it is like to push the limits.

During the teen years, one of my sons began hanging with the wrong crowd. He felt like my rules were too restrictive. There was some aggression. He left and I did not hear from him for a few weeks. Meanwhile, he got into all sorts of mischief that had the local police requesting that I stop by the station. He eventually had to spend a night in jail. After that ordeal, I had no problems with him leaving and staying away. My other son was with a group of friends, but he was the only one who was brought in and questioned. He received a hearing and was ordered to complete community service hours. They did not like the consequences. Maintaining a stable base while your child discovers himself in the world demonstrates commitment. As parent leader you don't have to be perfect to be committed. Together we got through it.

Recreation

Enjoying family time is so important in establishing a healthy family unit despite the trauma of the past. Creating atmospheres and new memories that children can enjoy and talk freely with your undivided attention listening and answering back with follow up questions strengthens the bond. A limited budget did not define the amount of fun we had. We had crossword and word search contests. We had loads of fun playing Monopoly, Connect Four and Checkers. With preteens, I had to forego the week long luxury vacations for the five of us because it was more important to me that I provide a safe environment for them to live and go to school. When they graduated, that safe place was also useful for them to attend college and find employment. Don't buy into the lie that there is no safe place. Pray and let God lead you. "But all who listen to me will live in peace, untroubled by fear of harm." Proverbs 1:33.

The park was our favorite hangout when the children were young. I would come home from work, change clothes and load their bikes in the car and go. As they grew older, I chose to pack lunches and head out to the forest preserves. We have rented a suite in Wisconsin or a local hotel room for a change of scenery. The times when I was around but not mentally present because I was working on a project (like this book) or taking a class, I noticed their impatience. I asked questions and established eye contact for a short while. I asked for more grace.

What does your family time of recreation look like? It can be as simple or as extravagant as your budget allows. More importantly, take the time to do it and be present. Create memories that last a lifetime.

CHAPTER SEVEN

Practice Self Care

> "Don't be afraid, for I am with you. Don't be discouraged, for I am your God. I will strengthen you and help you. I will hold you up with my victorious right hand." Isaiah 41:10 New Living Translation

I say to myself I am believing God, but I am starting to see more of my scalp when the stylist gives me the mirror to see how I like my new hairstyle. I have knots in my stomach as each day unfolds … praying that I hear no more bad news. Everything around me is falling apart. I am terrified about raising our children alone. The voices around me are yelling things that do not connect with my soul.

"Just be still. Time heals all wounds."

"Don't cry!"

"Be strong and hold on! Keep preaching and singing."

"Do what we say and you will be fine."

I was mentally and physically beat down from searching and following the methods of others as I attempted to carry the heavy load of my family. I realized I was not okay with the status quo and exalting the experiences of others above my own did not work. We are unwise when we compare ourselves to others. Our perspective and our situation is unique regardless how similar someone else's tragedy is. There are sacrifices that you may be willing to make that others bypass. I chose to deal with the ache in my heart. Acknowledging when life no longer works is a sign that something needs to change.

Your day may consist of childcare, career, school events, preparing meals, Bible class and maybe an occasional fun event. Maybe you don't plan. You just go when you want and where you want. You may not have the option to deny overtime ... working and working. If you keep going, no one will ever suspect that you are *just* functioning.

You are mildly depressed and feeling guilty about the choices you have made. You allow those negative emotions to hold you back from moving on. According to Dr. Colbert, in his book *Deadly Emotions*, the body cannot tell the difference between emotional and physical pain. Prolonged negative emotions affect our physical body leading to chronic illness and disease.

Talk therapy is a fantastic way to release the pressure of responsibility. Reach out to a friend for a light-hearted conversation. If you find that you want to talk to someone who is objective and detached from the situation, consider hiring a coach. A coach specializes in guiding and supporting you through to positive outcomes. As Les Brown says, "It's hard to see the picture when you are in the picture frame."

The frame

When I get off the train from work, I walk faster as I am anxious to see my children. They are smiling and not ready to leave the caregiver. Mrs. Bea asks about my day. The pain of the broken expectations of my life at this point devours me. She listens while I cry and talk for hours daily. There is much that she can say, being the age of my own mother, but she does not. She does not pretend or condescend to know my thoughts and feelings. When I stop, she reminds me who I am (and whose I am) and speaks words of comfort to my soul. She provides a safe non-judgmental space until I find my own answers.

My original idea of the perfect family does not work and I fail my children. My head is arguing with my heart. She and her daughters take care of me and my children for several years. There will be other lessons along this journey. But these valuable moments help me gain strength and clarity about myself, my reality and the next steps I must take for my family.

Is there someone with a solid disposition you can confide in? Bear in mind, it is self-destructive to be vulnerable to people who do not have your best interests in mind.

How do you measure your growth inside of your story? Try to avoid some common depression-laden death traps. You may be tempted to compare your life's work with people who do not have the same responsibilities as you. There is no comparison to someone who is not a parent. Chasing other people's ideas of happiness is also a dead end. We attempt to duplicate and medicate rather than walk fully as the person we are created to be. Insecure people cannot love you to life because they do not yet know their worth.

The value of physical touch is healing. Being a survivor of abuse, I have not been fond of touch. I show affection to my children at times by kissing them and telling them I love them, and I ask for lots of hugs. But honestly, it is a deliberate action.

The New York Times reported that a massage can reduce levels of stress hormones, such as cortisol, improve joint function and reduce pain in people with osteoarthritis. It also temporarily reduces muscle soreness after hard exercise and speeds healing of sore, overworked muscles by reducing inflammation. Allowing someone to work out your joints is exhilarating. Recently, I signed up for a chair massage at work. While I was in the chair with my face pressed against the opening, I was thinking, "How did I get here?" But as the massage therapist started on my back, I closed my eyes and took a deep breath. I focused on my breathing as I felt the sensations. It was gentle, and not as aggressive as I had imagined. In fact, as I relaxed, it was a wonderful experience. Growth and healing.

We cannot avoid all stress; however, it must be managed. Carrying the responsibility of a family gets very heavy, even when you attempt to lay your burdens down at the altar. And remember the body does not know the difference between emotional and physical pain so it may attempt to transfer your emotional pain to the physical, if it isn't getting the attention it needs.

Diet and exercise extends your life by increasing your energy and strengthening your core. You are so worth your time and attention. Be good to yourself.

If you shut down and never acknowledge your struggles, your child may not be free to express his emotions freely with you. He may turn to the other voices in the world for validation and acceptance of his weaknesses. When I broke my foot and had to stay off of it for three months, my children, now older, resembled the traffic at a train station during rush hour. They had no problem waking up for school and going to their jobs. I had the privilege of seeing our daily routines demonstrated without me in it. I have considered many times that if I am no longer here on earth, my children will be alone. Children recite our speech and model our actions. Now knowing they are equipped to take on some responsibility helps me to adjust and prioritize my own need for proper rest and relaxation.

How do you handle stress? The American Heart Association reports that the number one cause of death is heart disease and long periods of stress. You may choose to take walks during your lunch hour or while the children are in school. Take the opportunity to embrace what is and shape what will be. Organization is key to maximizing your energy, time and efforts.

Studies also show that the number one cause of stress is money. U.S. Census Bureau reported that 33% of single parents are more likely than any other group to fall into poverty. Procrastination is costly. You can choose to be wise about investing your resources. Be intentional about practicing self-care. Invest in your personal growth. There is a better life awaiting you.

CHAPTER EIGHT

Calming the Chaos of Your Child's Emotions

> A cheerful heart is good medicine, but a broken spirit saps a person's strength. Proverbs 17:22 New Living Translation

Children are well aware of our moods and the tones in our speech. They notice the hint of frustration in our body language. They are experts at touching the tender places of our heart, and they become very good at learning how to get what they want from us. Some children try very hard to get our attention. Why should it be so hard?

Even if your child never voices his fear, he most likely feels your anxiety. His life is also different if he lives with the other parent. He may express it at school through behavioral challenges. He may have nightmares and painful memories. He may become withdrawn.

The truth of the matter is, if you do not acknowledge your pain, you won't fully acknowledge the painful experiences of your child. Furthermore, if you mask or do not acknowledge your pain, you cannot calm the chaos in his heart. Take courage and build a bridge to emotionally secure your household.

It is painful for our children to see our eyes light up with excitement about lesser things. Don't tempt your child to be envious of that thing that has you so intoxicated. They will go out to fill the void with things that do not satisfy.

What if your child were to say:

> *Your new relationship has you skipping around and yet you have only known that person for a short while. Yet, without almost no eye contact, you give me orders about cleaning your house and what I should eat for dinner. You give me birthday parties, but it is more for you and your friends with no real contact with me. I hear you tell your friends that you need time to yourself or you "cannot wait until these kids are grown."*

Even if they don't say it, chances are you have been exhaling that for years now. Take a breath …

Young adults need your guidance in figuring out the world. There are no automatics. Threatening to kick them out without being prepared could backfire.

Is your child thinking, "I don't want to get in trouble, but maybe if I do, then you will come looking for me. Just maybe you will stop and consider that I need your attention too."

We not only give our attention to people, but organizations

and our jobs. We give ourselves wholeheartedly to church. We spend hours there without addressing the dysfunction in our home. We return inspired with no strategy to tackle the insecurities our children face in this big world. Dismissive and permissive, we choose not to be present emotionally.

Our children feel it, even if they don't say it. Let me be their voice:

"When I desire that you console me or assure me, you cannot be found. Your body is present, but you hide emotionally."

"You isolate yourself in your job. It is your favorite excuse for not showing up. And when you get home, you shut down."

"You do not notice the pain in my eyes as I consider giving in to the pressure of trying drugs or negative associations. I hurt too and no one seems to care. I am confused by your condition. Sometimes I think you are weak and one more traumatic event will separate us forever. But then other times, I am angry because just when I want to feel sorry for you, you choose to neglect me once again. I fear losing you to death, but in some ways, I feel like I have already lost you."

I know that hurts to hear but imagine how your child feels.

The American Academy of Pediatrics reports that adolescents from age 5-14 commit suicide more often and experience relationship problems with family members. The thought of adolescent children committing suicide is heartbreaking. Children are our future. They are supposed to discover wonderful opportunities to learn and grow, buy us gifts from their fortune, and take care of us when we get older. Apart from any personal gain, it's gut-wrenching that the gifts they bring to the world could be quenched so early.

In 1 Samuel, Chapter 16, the prophet Samuel was coming to the house of Jesse to anoint the next king among his sons. What an exciting day! Jesse prepared his older sons and the prophet said, God did not choose any of these. He asked if there was another son. Jesse never considered his youngest son, David who kept the sheep. Jesse called for him while he was out working in the field. Today, there are parents who also lack insight to the assignment on their child. Parents get caught up in their pre-determined plans whether it is a career, the military, an association, club or a particular school. You are responsible for raising your child to sow richly into the earth. Because we fail to see and nurture those gifts, our children often do not learn to appreciate themselves either. That can balloon into quiet despair that is only heard when it's too late.

Your child needs clear direction from you, especially after trauma. Your communication provides a safe place in his heart. He does not have to live in fear that something will happen again, or if it does, he can be confident that you will be there. You may feel like your child does not understand. He does. Even if you do not feel you can provide calm in the midst of a storm, this should be your goal. That creates trust within your family.

CHAPTER NINE

The Other Parent

> "Submit to God, and you will have peace; then things will go well for you." Job 22:21 New American Standard Bible

There may be conflicts when scheduling time with the other parent. Or perhaps the other parent is not coming around much or at all. In addition, many abusive relationships do not end on amicable terms because there is loss of control. Sometimes too much communication can restart the cycle of manipulation to return to the toxic relationship. There are parents who commit, if not verbally, mentally to staying involved with the life of the other parent outside of the relationship in the same fashion as they were inside of the relationship. It is a form of mental cruelty and self-destruction as you give main stage attention to the other parent's romantic relationships. There is also fear that maybe the other parent will forget the child because they have other children. At other times, the child is used as a rag doll between two egotistical people who refuse to consider that their behavior is suffocating to a child.

I never heard anyone's perspective inside of the church on the transition of going "cold turkey" without sex after being married for several years. It is hard. Very hard. Some people assume that if there is desire, that should be enough to sustain the marriage. When he left (and returned) all those times, sex is what kept me emotionally connected ... and pregnant. But if I wanted to provide my children with a better life, I knew I had to stay focused. Some men view "barefoot and pregnant" as a form of weakness to gain some weird advantage. But eventually I could no longer accept being scattered in my emotions as I had been all those years. I had to learn to think to live rather than allowing my decisions to be dictated by biology or emotion.

After he walked out the last time, I did not want to be around my ex-husband. After years of desperate pursuit, I finally accepted him for not what I wanted him to be, but for who he is. That was growth. Thanks to prayer and deliverance, as well as psychotherapy sessions, I developed a realistic view of the danger of being vulnerable to someone who continually schemed to deceive and harm me. Rather than see him as a victim of unfortunate circumstances, I saw him as a person continually making decisions against me.

As time went on, I did not want my children to have a relationship with their father based on whether I would re-enter the relationship. I wondered if it was possible for him to have a sense of duty to care for them as their responsible parent. The court provided a safe neutral place. We agreed that he would visit the children while they were with their caregiver.

The Illinois courthouse have mediation and personnel to help parents communicate during separation and after divorce. There is also assistance for unmarried parents. I recently sat inside of a courtroom where I saw my past life played out by other parents. It all became clear to me as I watched. The court understands that emotions are on edge regardless of your race, where you live, rich or poor, beautiful or ugly, churched or unchurched. This service by the justice department works for the best interests of the child. This person that you once loved and share a child with becomes "the enemy." In the courtroom, parents argue over the care of infants to children the age of 17. Some parents do not consider that because of your child in common, you and the other parent are connected for as long as the child is alive so you might as well fasten your seatbelt and get comfortable. It is possible that you may need each other should your child have a health challenge.

Also consider:

You contribute to the harm of your child by using negative language against the other parent in the presence of the child.

You contribute to the child's ill health when you make prideful decisions about visitation and withholding information such as location of residence and job information, if it is not warranted.

You make attorneys wealthy when you cannot agree on even the simple things. That money could be used on the care of the child.

You influence your child's behavior even during your absence.

While you may have become great at functioning with a bitter heart, your children may fail in school and in life because of these bitter roots.

Whoever you become romantically involved with must be prepared to get an earful of your frustration. They also directly affect your children as what they say, do and feel towards your children are part of their environment and generally their psyche.

As time moves on, there was no way for me to shield our children from his neglect. I can count on one hand the visits. On one occasion, I made my daughter go with her brothers to visit him and his wife. By this time, she was of age. My daughter finally confessed, "Mom, I am uncomfortable because I do not know him." It is very painful to listen to my children ask questions about why their Dad was not active in their lives. Rather than trying to fulfill both roles and fail miserably, I decided to focus more on becoming the best mother that I could be. That involved embracing personal development and becoming a student of my children. When they were younger, they called him expecting to hear from him. Now that they are older, he calls them expecting to hear from them.

Do not deny your child access to the other half of their identity if at all possible. Some of the turmoil in our relationships is not directly because of our children. Regardless how much pain and anger the other parent is causing you and your child, your child will love them. Give up trying to turn your child's opinion away from his parent. He will resent you for it.

I was told that I would never make it raising our children alone. His absence throughout the years made it seem like he was standing back and waiting for us to fail. The harder it became, the harder I prayed. Many days I considered how cruel his childhood must have been that it robbed him of the courage to have a real exchange with his children. There have been times through the years that his presence would have made things easier, especially during our son's illness or when I was duped out of a housing deal and we became homeless. I was earning less than half of my previous salary while working in the school near my son. I spent many of those nights watching over my children as we lay in cots next to strangers. This set back was harder on my son as I attempted to keep his medical appointments nearby. On payday weekends, I would rent a hotel room so that we could take baths. Eventually, I was able to save enough to secure a place to live with better schools. After receiving help for my son, doors were opened for me to return and work at the same building that I had previously worked before my son's accident. At every turn, God has proven his faithfulness.

As our children grow, I celebrate the wholeness of them. Our children have mannerisms like their father and they are a beautiful representation of us both. I never wanted them to be hindered in life because they feel fragmented. There are too many other ideologies in this world that fight against them or try to fill the empty places. It is possible to create an environment of stable unconditional emotional support allowing them to find peace. Help is available.

Of course, my children were affected, like any child, by

the absence of their father. Nonetheless, I was somewhat puzzled when my twenty-year old son asked me why I chose not to reconcile with his father because of the amount of time that had passed. While some children cope well with the way life has turned out, others hope that there will be reconciliation. Choose to listen to your child's perspective concerning his family. What may seem like an attack is really an expression of their pain and often it is the child inside them asking questions they were unable to frame earlier. Check in often to maintain the free flow of conversation. Your child may speak highly of the other parent. Encourage them to do so. It is important in accepting their own individuality. Listen even if she says something about you that you do not want to hear. The parent who is most involved often becomes the target of ridicule, anger and other negative emotions that sometimes prove temporary as the child sees you are committed to him for the long haul. The negative behavior may be for a season and affect other siblings or other places like school or the neighborhood. This is difficult. Renew your mind and stabilize your emotions. Do not retreat. Take courage. You have everything inside of you to get through the rough times *together.*

CHAPTER TEN

Premature Intimacy

> Therefore, since we are surrounded by such a huge crowd of witnesses to the life of faith, let us strip off every weight that slows us down, especially the sin that so easily trips us up. And let us run with endurance the race God has set before us. Hebrews 12:1 New Living Translation

Sometimes we get romantically involved too soon and get caught in a tailspin of unstable emotions. We look for what is familiar so we can resume our ideal life without considering what went wrong in the last relationship. We come off as desperate and incomplete rather than available and whole. We look for someone, anyone, to come and take away the pain of rejection or abandonment. We subscribe to what has been told to us about our story. We open ourselves up to more risk of the same treatment. If what is familiar did not work, why do you want more of the same?

Our unrealistic expectations may also put the other person in an uncomfortable position. They may be interested in learning about you and your children, but they may not be ready to take on the commitment of being a surrogate parent. We turn on the water hose of personal data and give immediate access to people who have not earned it.

When you meet someone when you are in the state of brokenness, you highlight the pain of your deepest wound. It becomes the prototype for what you scrutinize in future friendships. You say, "Well, as long as he doesn't hit me, he is a good man." With this narrow focus, you will not realize that you may not be compatible in other important areas. Yes, you can go buy new clothes, curl your hair, or move to another state, but you don't change the way you see yourself by accident. If you live out of pain, it attracts more pain.

GROWTH GEM: What are the other qualities you desire in a person? What are your top three non-negotiable values in a relationship?

Sometimes in an attempt to avoid what we do not want, we shut down. We close off our vulnerability because we fail to consider what we do want. Don't give up. We can heal, overcome and grow into healthy connections. Take the time to evaluate your needs. This may mean going solo rather than serial dating. Choose to invest the time to evaluate the events in your past relationships. How are they the same? What is different? Are you headed in the same direction? You will discover the truth about yourself and your need for companionship. Will you settle, or will you wait for your non-negotiable values, even if it means being alone for a while?

Six months after my husband departed, I returned to

school to complete a business management program. My daughter was eight months old. I was assigned a financial aid adviser. He made sure my paperwork was complete. He also proved to be a great listener. Eventually we become good friends. Because he lived across town, we did not see him very often, but he provided bright sunshine to us during a very dark period.

In my opinion, it was much too soon for me to consider another romantic interest, which is what it felt like because it was positive attention. I honored my marriage vow before God until my divorce, but I did accept his beautiful roses and the delicious meals he provided for me and the children. He met my mother and Mrs. Bea. I talked for hours and he listened. It felt wonderful, but I was deeply wounded and simply could not provide the balance he needed because I had no clarity about my life. To be honest, it was overwhelming. But was God inviting him into my life to make me forget my terrible past? Can one person bear the burden of another person's past, especially, if they have not dealt with it themselves?

I reached out to my pastor, for clarity and validation, about this man's interest and he said, "Does he know you have T-H-R-E-E children?" I answered yes. He asked again implying that it was hard to believe that the guy would be genuinely interested because of the number of children I had. Was I being placed in a new category: unmatchable? In any case, I asked if he would meet him. He agreed. My loyalty to my pastor was solid and I trusted his opinion more than I trusted myself at that point. I wanted him to help me scrutinize him. By the way, I failed to pray about it, nor did he tell me to pray about it.

When I involved my new friend/possible romantic interest in my church affairs trying to prove his good intentions to others, it caused strife in our friendship. I realized belatedly it probably would have been better had I not mentioned him at all. On the first night of his visit, I was instructed to step back and allow him to choose which woman he wanted. He was introduced to another young lady on another occasion. I was married all those years and hadn't realized some churches were the new place for a "hook up." Later, I received a call of apology. It troubled me deeply because I begged this well-educated man who lived across town to meet the people who were supposed to look out for me. Our "friendship" beamed the light again on the presence of unhealthy codependent relationships I had allowed to enter my life as I sought identity and purpose. Scripture says let thine eyes look right on.

After a while, he proposed to me and an announcement was made in front of the church. It seemed like it would have been perfect as proof that he was sincere. Meanwhile, the accusations being made from the pulpit confirmed what I was beginning to see about the people in my life. They said they loved us, but the silence and the distance I felt was so painful. More importantly, there was much work to be done about my own distorted thinking. Also, it hurt me so much that I had even inadvertently caused pain to my friend. It was a valuable lesson; I learned to commit to accept people as they are. In the words of Maya Angelou, "When people show you who they are, believe them."

A few years after my divorce, after I had started learning to take control of my own life, we randomly talked on the phone. We missed him. I missed him. He helped us move into our new place, offering the same kindness. So, yes, at thirty, I found myself afraid to tell my mother that I was pregnant again. I was so put off, I left the car running the entire time I was in the doctor's office.

It was difficult caring for three children while maintaining a demanding job. My career was soaring. At the same time, I was embarrassed as a minister and former praise leader. I wondered what they would say at my previous church in my absence. It would seem that the accusations flying over the pulpit at the beginning of our friendship were true. I chose the story that this kid was created out of love and life comes from God. We choose what things mean.

It was a confusing place as I was attempting to face the music of my life, on my terms. I would listen to Pastor Angie Ray every morning at 5:30 a.m. and pray strong deliverance prayers. Our baby had to stay a few extra days in the hospital. I kept saying, singing in my heart: "Lord make me over. I wanna be made over." When I brought him home, God comforted my heart with Psalm 32:1. Blessed is the one whose transgressions are forgiven and sins are covered. Today we co-parent a very intelligent young teenager.

In time, I learned to make better decisions about my new perceived value and role as a woman of God, a committed mother of four, a valued employee and business owner. It is not always who we choose but to whom we answer. The idea of waiting on someone to help me care for my children is the general assumption in most religious settings. It is tempting, but I was not sure I wanted to share my children and cause more disruption in their lives. They are depending on me for stability. Getting to know someone takes time and even more time after a traumatic event. During the eighteen years of raising my children, I have met men who are very interested in getting close to me, but only ask about my children briefly. I was invited to go on cruises and to travel to exotic beaches. I asked, "Who will be around for my grade school children?" He asked, "Where is their father?" Looking ahead, would this mean a constant battle of choosing between time with him and them, or me having to do a "hard sell" about why he should accept us as a package?

Another time I learned through a coincidence that one guy I met at a prayer breakfast was listed as a convicted sex offender. He had an impressive background of military service and strong family heritage. The doors of the church are open to everyone so this alone cannot be the measurement of whether someone is suitable for you. I asked if it was true because he had been around my children and had not shared the details with me. It was not my place to judge, but there was no place for him in our lives.

One guy I dated scanned my daughter's body with his eyes as we were leaving his office. I just happened to look back. He is the same man who asked my children if he could marry me. He did not have any children which was attractive to me. But a man without children would have to learn the mindset of a father in a household of young children. In addition, as parent leader, I had to consider my teenage daughter and the timing of pursuing a relationship. My conduct could be a distraction to her. We cannot close our eyes to truth and expect a fairytale ending.

Overall, when I consider the days of attending singles events and waiting for someone to come and rescue me from my "single" parent role, I inwardly shake my head in defense. I choose rather to work on building my faith and asking myself the hard questions about patterns like attracting the same type of guy with a different name. What area do I need to work on in my life that would make his heart safely trust in me as stated in Proverbs 31:11? Am I choosing from a place of wholeness or deficiency? When the right man comes along, will I have done the work to have value added conversation? Deciding that I am not willing to put my children in an uncomfortable position in the home I provide for them comes from a place of growth: P.T.S.D. Parents Transforming with Strength and Determination.

My sons, who are now both in their twenties and are college graduates, ask if I am open to meeting someone as they attach themselves in relationships. I am happy to have a voice of influence to encourage them to pursue healthy friendships. My prayer has always been that God would direct them to their spouses so they can create strong and healthy marriages. Having a good education, pursuing what they enjoy while earning a great income for themselves is a priority. They are on track by God's grace. When the time is right to choose, they will attract who they are. While I cannot choose for them, I can build them up with strength and vigor about themselves as young adults, keep the lines of communication open and encourage them to seek positive examples of marriage. For our children after trauma, the best relationships are guided until the age of accountability. Create an environment that discourages hiding or keeping secrets. There is no need when you are committed to the well-being of your child.

What desires do you have for the future relationships of your children? What decisions are you willing to make as a model today so that your children can live an abundant life going forward?

While I continue to seize what is possible for me, my focus is on legacy building and completing the projects on my heart. Time is so precious. The one God has for me will find me working in the field as I live out my calling and purpose pursuing wholeness. Until then, there is plenty of excitement helping my children grow.

CHAPTER ELEVEN

This is not the life I planned.

> I'm not saying that I have this all together, that I have it made. But I am well on my way, reaching out for Christ, who has so wondrously reached out for me. Friends, don't get me wrong: by no means do I count myself an expert in all of this, but I've got my eye on the goal, where God is beckoning us onward-to Jesus. I'm off and running, and I'm not turning back. Philippians 3:12-14 The Message

This is not the life I planned either, but we must go on. I am here to encourage you to use what you have in your hands. You are more than enough to complete this journey to wholeness. Regardless of how it may appear, parenting is a leadership position. It has the same requirements as world leaders: focus, courage, tenacity, passion and vision.

If you choose to lead in fear, scarcity and poverty, your child may get stuck too. They will not have the skills necessary to adapt to a changing world. I recognize that if my children are going to make it in this world, I must plant seeds of unconditional love, courage and fortitude. If I build them up on the inside, I can assure you that the outside world won't affect them as much. An African Proverb states, "If there is no enemy within, the enemy outside can do us no harm." I choose to do what I can to place them in an environment that is supportive of their efforts.

There are survival skills we learn going through tough times. They become transferable skills. I train to run marathons by faith with the Kingdom Running Club. I was never athletic, but I wanted to break the cycle of sickness and disease in my family. The discipline I learn affects my diet and other areas of my life. I have now completed four half marathons and six 5ks. It is beyond anything I have ever attempted, and it boosts my confidence to new levels and changes my approach to how I see challenges. Much like training to run a race, raising children is an assignment that takes patience: one step at a time. With God all things are possible.

Sometimes your journey may take route to an unfamiliar place that requires absolute faith in God, a place that allows you to officially disconnect from the toxic environments you have previously known. The new place may allow you to establish friendships that inspire you to hope again. It may give your child an opportunity to see life from another vantage point. It may give them access to people who seek to learn about who he is as an individual without the baggage of whatever choices his parents made.

Your child deserves a stable environment free and clear of emotional and physical abuse. No blame. No coping as if we have no choice. You can take one hundred percent responsibility for your life.

You will never know if you do not trust the leading of God to take care of you and your family. I remember thinking, there are no "good" food places in this new environment. We would drive back to the city and get seasoned, greasy food. It began to make my stomach hurt, but I did not think much about it until I learned that the restaurant did not change their grease. It was an opportunity to adopt a new mindset. I compared for the first time the food desert in the city to the plenteous vegetation we drove by on the farms to get to the processed foods we were used to. You will find that if you persist in keeping an old mindset, you will quickly be snatched out of abundance. You will fall back into the dungeon of your old mindset and comfort zone. It is uncomfortable to grow so "get comfortable with being uncomfortable" until uncomfortable is your new normal. Pastor and author R.C. Blakes, Jr. once said on his Periscope broadcast, "The loneliest place is not at the top; it is in between the levels." Grow on purpose WITH purpose!

I have been criticized for the way I raise my children, leaving me to wonder if I was capable or crazy. We attended prayer meetings when they were younger. It is important for my children to hear the voice of God above the noise. Along with the turmoil in my household growing up, my Dad took me and my brothers to prayer meetings. The women wailing vexed my soul. I said I would not return when I got old enough. But I believe those seeds of prayer were planted deep inside of me. It has been my strength in my adult life. I have not always made the best decisions, but prayer brings me back to safety and I'm very grateful.

I invest intentional energy in parenting because I am curious to know how liberating it would be if a child did not live with the narrow belief that the world is bad after trauma. This can lead to rejecting all of the resources God has provided for his children. I want to know what it looks like without hearing the voices of mediocrity while their spirit yearns to create something that does not yet exist. I want them to journey on a path that is beyond the tradition of cold love steeped in manipulation and learn how powerful God has made them to be. They are made in his image and after his likeness, fulfilling the plan that God himself has planted in their hearts.

Stewardship is what we as parent leaders do as we present our child back to God. And if there is ever some insecurity about who they are not or what they do not have, our children can know how important they are to us. They can know how important they are to the world. And I pray that it propels them to go as far as God will take them.

Some of us live out of regret. We say, if I had not done that, or met him/her, my life would be so much better. We create scenarios with our imagination about what could have happened without the trauma, never realizing that we are robbing ourselves of the treasures of wisdom from what did happen. Your thoughts dominate your actions. Don't miss this season.

Listen to your life. God in his sovereignty orchestrates

our existence in a beautiful musical suite if we choose to yield. Life is more than motion … it is music. We do not have to live by the default of broken expectation. When we take courage, pursue the help we need to renew our minds and develop our faith, we discover that inside our pain is the promise that remains throughout our journey. No man is an island. We all need support. I am grateful for the lessons, and I am happy to share them with you.

The gifts of my children have exposed me to opportunities that have made my life richer. This is not the life I planned. But this is the life God planned. And it is more valuable than I could have ever imagined. God has avenues and revenues we know nothing about. May you find the golden nuggets in your story. You can be a parent transforming with strength and dominion.

11 Keys to Positive Parenting After Trauma Checklist

1. Assess the trauma in your life. - You can't change what has happened, but you can courageously choose to confront your emotions and resolve them in your heart so that you can be fully available to your child.

2. You can do this! – It is possible for you to raise healthy productive adults after trauma.

3. Who are you now after the trauma? - Identify and examine the beliefs that keep you from moving forward to the life you desire.

4. Spiritual Renewal - You have access to the Source of all wisdom, knowledge and understanding: the equation for healing and wholeness.

5. Importance of Language - Speak what you want to see in yourself, your children, your home, and your career.

6. Embrace your authority. – Be proactive in the areas that help to develop your child's sense of self-worth.

7. Practice Self Care. - Be intentional to complete your assignment with joy. Feed your spirit, soul and body with what fills you up spiritually, emotionally and physically.

8. Calm the chaos of your child's emotions. - Acknowledge and encourage your child's expression of the unfortunate events and lead him to wholeness.

9. The other parent - Make the remainder of your life about the present and not the past. Change your view of the other parent in a way that empowers your child to receive what they need from you both. Most of what you do as a parent is for your child. Support your child's healthy self-image.

10. Premature intimacy – You cannot give from a place of lack. Realize your emotional strengths and weaknesses and commit to do the work for selecting and building healthy connections going forward.

11. This is not the life I planned. - But this is the life God planned. Go forth with strength and dominion and live your life of purpose.

References

Burton, V.,(2004) Listen to Your Life: Following Your Unique Path to Extraordinary Success: Waterbrook Press, Print

Colbert, M.D., D., (2006) Deadly Emotions: Understand the Mind-Body-Spirit Connection that Can Heal or Destroy You, Thomas Nelson Publishers, Print

Copeland, Christy, (2013) My Promise to You Discography

Warren, R., (2002) The Purpose-Driven Life: What on Earth Am I Here for? Grand Rapids, Mich.: Zondervan, Print

Darling Ph.D., N. (2014) Authoritative vs. Authoritarian Parenting Style, Psychology Today, Retrieved from: https://www.psychologytoday.com/blog/thinking-about-kids/201409/authoritative-vs-authoritarian-parenting-style

Darling Ph.D., N. (2010) The Language of Parenting: Legitimacy of Parental Authority, Psychology Today,

Retrieved from:
https://www.psychologytoday.com/blog/thinking-about-kids/201001/the-language-parenting-legitimacy-parental-authority

Sheftall, A.H., Asti, L., Horowitz, L.M. Felts, A., Fontanella, C.A., Campo, J.V., Bridge, J.A. (2016) Suicide in Elementary School-Aged Children and Early Adolescents, American Academy of Pediatrics, VOLUME 138 / ISSUE 4, Retrieved from
http://pediatrics.aappublications.org/content/138/4/e20160436

Let's Continue the Conversation online.

Your support is greatly appreciated. Please leave a review.

You are invited to explore your personal journey with us at our next Wellness Workshop.

To learn more about our wellness workshops, events and speaking engagements:
https://www.leaderswellnesssuite.com

Connect with us on social media:
https://www.instagram.com/thecoachingwell/
https://www.facebook.com/thecoachingwell/

For Confidential Wellness Coaching, schedule
https://bit.ly/booklws

For questions or more information: email us at
info@leaderswellnesssuite.com

About the Author

Christy Copeland is a speaker, parent advocate, warrior domestic violence survivor and your certified breakthrough coach. Christy is the founder and executive director of Leaders Wellness Suite LLC, a faith-based personal development company providing individual transformational coaching and wellness workshops to parents who choose trauma recovery. She hosts P.T.S.D. (Parents Transforming with Strength & Dominion) Podcast on iTunes, Spotify and Stitcher Radio. For more than twenty years, Christy has served business leaders in the corporate sector of manufacturing, banking and law. She is a recording artist and a marathon finisher. Christy resides just outside of Chicago, Illinois.